Diesterwegs
Neusprachliche
Bibliothek

Charles Webb

The Graduate

Edited and annotated
by
Gerd Ulmer

DIESTERWEG

Charles Webb was born in 1939 in San Francisco. He was educated at Williams College, Massachusetts, where he graduated in American history and literature. *The Graduate* was his first novel; since then he has published *Love, Roger, The Marriage of a Young Stockbroker* (which was made into a successful film) and *The Abolitionist of Clark Gable Place* (1976).

He has held numerous jobs, including that of a stockroom help at a department store in California. Charles Webb plays the flute; he is married and has two sons.

Published by arrangement with New American Library, New York, N.Y.

Druck A [17] / Jahr 2009
Alle Drucke der Serie A sind im Unterricht parallel verwendbar.

Umschlagfoto: Cinetext/Bildarchiv
Umschlagkonzeption: Blum-Design und Kommunikation, Hamburg
Umschlagrealisation: Harald Thumser, Frankfurt
Satz: Stahringer Satz GmbH, Grünberg
Druck und Bindung: westermann druck GmbH, Braunschweig

ISBN 978-3-425-**04834**-5

Part One

1

Benjamin Braddock graduated from a small Eastern college* on a day in June. Then he flew home. The following evening a party was given for him by his parents. By eight o'clock most of the guests had arrived but Benjamin had not yet come down from his room. His father called up from the foot of the stairs but there was no answer. Finally he hurried up the stairs and to the end of the hall.

"Ben?" he said, opening his son's door.

"I'll be down later," Benjamin said.

"Ben, the guests are all here," his father said. "They're all waiting."

"I said I'll be down later."

Mr Braddock closed the door behind him. "What is it," he said.

Benjamin shook his head and walked to the window.

"What is it, Ben."

"Nothing."

"Then why don't you come on down and see your guests."

Benjamin didn't answer.

"Ben?"

"Dad," he said, turning around, "I have some things on my mind right now."

"What things."

"Just some things."

"Well can't you tell me what they are?"

"No."

Mr Braddock continued frowning* at his son a few more moments, glanced at his watch, then looked back at Benjamin. "Ben, these are our friends down there," he said. "My friends. Your mother's friends. You owe them a little courtesy*."

"Tell them I have to be alone right now."

"Mr Robinson's out in the garage looking at your new sports car. Now go on down and give him a ride in it."

to graduate from a college a college traditionally offers a broadly-based course, leading in four years to the academic title of Bachelor of Arts/Science (B.A./B.Sc.); to graduate is to gain the final diploma after the four year course **Eastern college** college in an Eastern state of the U.S.A. **to frown** to look angrily **courtesy** politeness

Benjamin reached into his pocket for a pair of shiny keys on a small chain. "Here," he said.

"What?"

"Give him the keys. Let him drive it."

"But he wants to see you."

"Dad, I don't want to see him right now," Benjamin said. "I don't want to see the Robinsons, I don't want to see the Pearsons, I don't want to see the ... the Terhunes."

"Ben, Mr Robinson and I have been practicing law together in this town for seventeen years. He's the best friend I have."

"I realize that."

"He has a client over in Los Angeles that he's put off seeing so he could be here and welcome you home from college."

"Dad—"

"Do you appreciate that?"

"I'd appreciate it if I could be alone!"

His father shook his head. "I don't know what's got into you," he said, "but whatever it is I want you to snap out of it* and march right on down there."

Suddenly the door opened and Benjamin's mother stepped into the room. "Aren't you ready yet?" she said.

"No."

"We'll be right down," his father said.

"Well what's wrong," she said, closing the door behind her.

"I am trying to think!"

"Come on, Ben," his father said. He took his arm and began leading him toward the door.

"Goddammit will you leave me alone!" Benjamin said. He pulled away and stood staring at him.

"Ben?" Mr Braddock said quietly, staring back at him, "don't you ever swear at your mother or me again."

Benjamin shook his head. Then he walked between them and to the door. "I'm going for a walk," he said. He stepped out into the hall and closed the door behind him.

He hurried to the head of the stairs and down but just as he had gotten to the front door and was about to turn the knob* Mr Terhune appeared out of the living room.

"Ben?" he said. "I want to shake your hand."

Benjamin shook it.

snap out of it stop being silly or bad-tempered **knob** round handle on the door

"Goddammit I'm proud of you," Mr Terhune said, still holding his hand.
Benjamin nodded. "Thank you," he said. "Now if you'll excuse me I'm going for a walk. I'll be back later."
Mrs Pearson appeared at the end of the hall. "Oh Benjamin," she said, smiling at him. She hurried to where he was standing and reached up to pull his head down and kiss him. "Benjamin?" she said. "I'm just speechless."
Benjamin nodded.
"Golly* you did a fine job back there*."
"I'm sorry to seem rude," Benjamin said, "but I'm trying to go on a walk right now."
Mr Robinson appeared at the end of the hall with a drink in his hand. He began grinning when he saw Benjamin and walked into the group of people surrounding him to shake his hand. "Ben, how in hell are you," he said. "You look swell*."
"I'm fine."
"Say, that's something out in the garage. That little Italian job* your old man gave you for graduation?"
"Oh how exciting," Mrs Pearson said.
"Let's go for a spin*," Mr Robinson said.
Benjamin reached into his pocket and pulled out the keys. "Can you work a foreign gearshift*?" he said, holding them out.
"What?"
"Do you know how to operate a foreign gearshift."
"Well sure," Mr Robinson said. "But I thought you'd take me for a little spin yourself."
"I can't right now," Benjamin said. "Excuse me." He reached for the doorknob and turned it, then pulled open the door. Just as he was about to step outside Mr and Mrs Carlson walked up onto the front porch*.
"Well here he is himself," Mrs Carlson said. She wrapped her arms around Benjamin and hugged* him. "Ben?" she said, patting one of his shoulders, "I hope you won't be embarrassed if I tell you I'm just awfully proud to know you."
"I won't," Benjamin said. "But I have some things on my mind at the moment and I'm—"
"Here's something for you," Mr Carlson said. He handed Benjamin a bottle wrapped with a red ribbon. "I hope they taught you to hold your liquor* back

golly exclamation for "God" **you did a fine job back there** you were really successful at college **swell** fine, very good **Italian job** *here* Italian car **spin** a short ride in the car **gearshift** *G* Gangschaltung **porch** verandah **to hug** to hold in one's arms **to hold one's liquor** to drink alcohol without showing signs of being drunk there." He threw his arm around Benjamin's shoulder and swept* him back inside the house.

Benjamin ducked* under his arm and set the bottle of liquor beside the door. "Look," he said. "Could you please let me go for my walk!"

"What?"

"I'm sorry not to be more sociable*," Benjamin said. "I appreciate everybody coming over but—"

"Now Ben," Mrs Carlson said as her husband removed her coat, "I want you to tell me all about this prize you won. It was for teaching, wasn't it?"

Benjamin grabbed the doorknob but before he could turn it his father appeared beside him and put his arm around him. "Let's get you fixed up with* a drink," he said.

"Dad?"

"Come on, Ben," his father said quietly. "You're making kind of a scene here."

"Then let me out!"

"Here we go," Mr Braddock said. He began leading him away from the door.

"All right!" Benjamin said. He walked ahead of his father and into the living room, shaking his head.

"Well Benjamin," a woman said.

Benjamin nodded.

"Aren't you just thrilled to death?"

He walked on through the room, nodding at several more guests, and into the dining room where there was a tray of bottles on the dining-room table and a bucket* of ice and some glasses. He selected one of the largest and poured it full of bourbon. Then he took several swallows, closed his eyes a moment and took several more. He refilled the glass to the top and turned around to see his mother standing in front of him.

"What's that," she said, frowning at the glass in his hand.

"This?"

"Yes."

"I don't know," he said. "Maybe it's a drink."

His mother turned her frown up to his face. "Ben, what's the trouble," she said.

"The trouble is I'm trying to get out of this house!"

"But what's on your mind."

"Different things, Mother."

to sweep back *here* to push back **to duck** to move with head down **sociable** ready to mix with people, friendly, talking to everyone **to get s.o. fixed up with s.th.** to provide s.o. with s.th.; to give s.o. s.th. **bucket** *G* Eimer; *here* (Eis-)kübel

"Well, can't you worry about them another time?"

"No."

Mrs Braddock reached for his drink. "Here," she said, taking it. "Come out to the kitchen for a minute."

Benjamin shook his head but followed her through the swinging door and into the kitchen. Mrs Braddock walked to the sink and poured out most of the drink, then filled the glass with water. "Can't you tell me what you're worried about?" she said, drying off the glass with a dish towel* beside the sink.

"Mother, I'm worried about different things. I'm a little worried about my future."

"About what you're going to do?"

"That's right."

She handed him back the glass. "Well you still plan to teach* don't you," she said.

"No."

"You don't?" she said. "Well what about your award*."

"I'm not taking it."

"You're not?"

"No."

"Well Ben," she said, "that doesn't sound very wise, to pass up* something you've spent four years working for."

Mr Terhune pushed into the kitchen carrying his drink. "I thought I saw you duck in here," he said. "Now let's have the lowdown* on that prize of yours."

"I'm not—"

"Tell him about it, Ben," his mother said.

"It's called the Frank Halpingham Education Award*," Benjamin said. "It's given by the college. It puts me through two years of graduate school if I decide to go into teaching."

"Well now why did they pick you," Mr Terhune said.

Benjamin didn't answer.

"He did some practice teaching back there," his mother said. "He's been an assistant teacher for two years. Last term they let him take a junior seminar* in American History."

dish towel cloth for drying glasses, cups, etc. **to teach** Benjamin would have to do an extra course of professional training (usually two years) to qualify as a teacher **award** financial support for further studies as a reward for academic success **to pass up** not to take **lowdown** all the facts **Frank Halpingham Education Award** a special award for teacher training; awards are often named after the person who gives the money for it, or in memory of a deceased person **junior seminar** seminar for third-year students

Mr Terhune sipped at his drink. "Well, have you got in any graduate schools yet?" he said.

"Yes."

"He's in Harvard* and Yale*," his mother said. "And what's that other one?"

"Columbia*."

Mr Terhune sipped at his drink again. "It sounds like you've got things pretty well sewed up*," he said.

Benjamin turned and walked quickly across the room to the back door. He opened it and walked out and to the edge of the swimming pool in the back yard. He stood staring down at the blue light rising up through the water for several moments before hearing the door open and bang shut behind him and someone walk across to where he was standing.

"Ben?" Mrs McQuire said. "I think your yearbook* is just unbelievable."

Benjamin nodded.

"Was there anyone who got his picture in there more times than you did?"

"Abe Frankel did."

Mrs McQuire shook her head. "What a fantastic record you made for yourself."

"Ben?" Mr Calendar came out beside the pool and shook Benjamin's hand. "Congratulations to you," he said.

"Have you seen Ben's yearbook?" Mrs McQuire said.

"Why no."

"Let's see if I can remember all the different things," she said. "Ben, you tell me if I miss any." She cleared her throat and counted them off on her fingers as she talked. "Captain of the cross-country team. Head of the debating club. First in his class."

"I wasn't first."

"Oh?"

"I tied Abe Frankel for first*."

"Oh," she said. "Now let's see what else. One of the editors of the school newspaper. Student teacher*. I'm running out of fingers. Social chairman of his house*. And that wonderful teaching award."

Harvard and **Yale** two of the most famous US universities, H. in Cambridge, Massachusetts; Y. in New Haven, Connecticut **Columbia** another famous university in New York City **to have things sewed up** to have everything so arranged that nothing can go wrong . **yearbook** book about the graduates of a particular year, recording their achievements, especially in sports, music, drama, etc. **to tie s.o. for first** to be no. 1 together with someone else, both having gained the same high marks **student teacher** as mentioned in the text before Benjamin was allowed to take a class (seminar) himself in the past two years to gain teaching practice **social chairman of his house** head of a committee elected to organize the social life of the students living in the same house; (students mainly live in large dormitory houses on the campus)

"Could I ask you a question," Benjamin said, turning suddenly toward her.
"Of course."
"Why are you so impressed with all those things."
"All the things you did?"
"Excuse me," Mr Calendar said, holding up his glass. "I think I'll find a refill." He turned around and walked back into the house.
"Could you tell me that, Mrs McQuire?"
She was frowning down into the bright blue water beside them. "Well," she said, "aren't you awfully proud of yourself? Of all those things?"
"No."
"What?" she said, looking up. "You're not?"
"I want to know why you're so impressed, Mrs McQuire."
"Well," she said, shaking her head. "I'm afraid—I'm afraid I don't quite see what you're driving at."
"You don't know what I'm talking about, do you."
"Well not exactly. No."
"Then why do you—why do you—" He shook his head. "Excuse me," he said. He turned around and walked back toward the house.
"Ben?" she called after him. "I'm afraid I haven't been much help, but if it makes any difference I just want so say I'm thrilled to pieces by all your wonderful achievements and I couldn't be prouder if you were my own son."
Benjamin opened the door leading into the living room. He walked through the room keeping his eyes ahead of him on the carpet until Mrs Calendar took his elbow.
"Ben?" she said. "I just think it's too terrific for words."
He walked past her and into the hall. Just as he got to the foot of the stairs his father came up behind him.
"Leave me alone."
"Ben, for God's sake what is it."
"I don't know what it is."
"Come here," Mr Braddock said. He took his arm and led him down the hall and into a bedroom. "Son?" he said, closing the door and locking it. "Now what is it."
"I don't know."
"Well something seems pretty wrong."
"Something is."
"Well what."
"I don't know!" Benjamin said. "But everything—everything is grotesque all of a sudden."

"Grotesque?"

"Those people in there are grotesque. You're grotesque."

"Ben."

"I'm grotesque. This house is grotesque. It's just this feeling I have all of a sudden. And I don't know why!"

"Ben, it's because you're all tied up in knots*."

Benjamin shook his head.

"Now I want you to relax."

"I can't seem to."

"Ben, you've just had four of the most strenuous* years of your life back there."

"They were nothing," Benjamin said.

"What?"

"The whole four years," he said, looking up at his father. "They were nothing. All the things I did are nothing. All the distinctions. The things I learned. All of a sudden none of it seems to be worth anything to me."

His father was frowning. "Why do you say that."

"I don't know," Benjamin said. He walked across the room to the door. "But I've got to be alone. I've got to think until I know what's happening to me."

"Ben?"

"Dad, I've got to figure this thing out before I go crazy," he said, unlocking the door. "I'm not just joking around either." He stepped back out into the hall.

"Ben?" Mr Robinson said, holding out his hand. "I've got a client waiting for me over in Los Angeles."

Benjamin nodded and shook his hand.

"Real proud of you boy," Mr Robinson said.

Benjamin waited till he had gone out the door, then turned around and walked upstairs and into his room. He closed the door behind him and sat down at his desk. For a long time he sat looking down at the rug*, then he got up and walked to the window. He was staring out at a light over the street when the door opened and Mrs Robinson stepped inside, carrying a drink and her purse*.

"Oh," she said. "I guess this isn't the bathroom is it."

"It's down the hall," Benjamin said.

She nodded but instead of leaving the room stood in the doorway looking at him.

to be tied up in knots to be confused **strenuous** full of hard work **rug** carpet **purse** *AE* handbag

"It's right at the end of the hall," Benjamin said.

Mrs Robinson was wearing a shiny* green dress cut very low across her chest, and over one of her breasts was a large gold pin.

"It's right at the end of the hall," Benjamin said.

"What?"

She smiled at him.

"Mrs Robinson," Benjamin said, shaking his head. "I'm kind of distraught* at the moment. Now I'm sorry to be rude but I have some things on my mind."

She walked across the room to where he was standing and kissed one of his cheeks.

"It's good to see you," Benjamin said. "The bathroom's at the end of the hall."

Mrs Robinson stood looking at him a moment longer, then turned around and walked to his bed. She seated herself on the edge of it and sipped at* her drink.

"How are you," she said.

"Look," Benjamin said. "I'm sorry not to be more congenial* but I'm trying to think."

Mrs Robinson had set her glass down on the rug. She reached into her purse for a package of cigarettes and held it out to Benjamin.

"No."

She took one for herself.

"Is there an ash tray in here?"

"No."

"Oh," she said, "I forgot. The track star* doesn't smoke." She blew out her match and set it down on the bedspread*.

Benjamin walked to his desk for a wastebasket and carried it to the bed. He picked up the match and dropped it in.

"Thank you."

He walked back to the window.

"What are you upset about," she said.

"Some personal things."

"Don't you want to talk about them?"

"Well they wouldn't be of much interest to you, Mrs Robinson."

She nodded and sat quietly on the bed smoking her cigarette and dropping ashes into the wastebasket beside her.

"Girl trouble?" she said.

"What?"

shiny *G* glänzend **I'm kind of distraught** I'm a little bit confused **to sip at** *G* nippen an **congenial** pleasant, nice **track star** running champion **bedspread** a bed cover

"Do you have girl trouble?"

"Look," Benjamin said. "Now I'm sorry to be this way but I can't help it. I'm just sort of disturbed* about things."

"In general," she said.

"That's right," Benjamin said. "So please." He shook his head and looked back out through the glass of the window.

Mrs Robinson picked up her drink to take a swallow* from it, then set it down and sat quietly until she was finished with her cigarette.

"Shall I put this out in the wastebasket?"

Benjamin nodded.

Mrs Robinson ground it out* on the inside of the wastebasket, then sat back up and folded her hands in her lap*. It was quiet for several moments.

"The bathroom's at the end of the hall," Benjamin said.

"I know."

She didn't move from the bed but sat watching him until finally Benjamin turned around and walked to the door. "Excuse me," he said. "I think I'll go on a walk."

"Benjamin?"

"What."

"Come here a minute."

"Look I'm sorry to be rude, Mrs Robinson. But I'm ..."

She held out her hands. "Just for a minute," she said.

Benjamin shook his head and walked back to the bed. She took both his hands in hers and looked up into his face for several moments.

"What do you want," he said.

"Will you take me home?"

"What?"

"My husband took the car. Will you drive me home?"

Benjamin reached into one of his pockets for the keys. "Here," he said. "You take the car."

"What?"

"Borrow the car. I'll come and get it tomorrow."

"Don't you want to take me home?" she said, raising her eyebrows.

"I want to be alone, Mrs Robinson. Now do you know how to work a foreign shift?"

She shook her head.

"You don't?"

"No."

sort of disturbed somehow confused or mixed up **swallow** *G* Schluck **to grind out a cigarette** to put out a cigarette **lap** *G* Schoß

Benjamin waited a few moments, then returned the keys to his pocket. "Let's go," he said.

Mr Braddock was standing in the front doorway saying goodbye to the Terhunes. "Mrs Robinson needs a ride home," Benjamin said. "I'll be right back."

"Wonderful party," Mrs Robinson said. She took her coat from a closet* beside the front door, put it on and followed Benjamin back through the house and out to the garage. He got into the car and started the engine and she got in beside him. "What kind of car is this," she said.

"I don't know."

He backed out* the driveway* and they drove without speaking the several miles between the Braddocks' home and the Robinsons'. Benjamin stopped by the curb* in front of her house. Mrs Robinson reached up to push some hair away from her forehead and turned in her seat to smile at him.

"Thank you," she said.

"Right."

She didn't move from her seat. Finally Benjamin turned off the engine, got out and walked around to open the door for her.

"Thank you," she said, getting out.

"You're welcome."

"Will you come in, please?"

"What?"

"I want you to come in till I get the lights on."

"What for."

"Because I don't feel safe until I get the lights on."

Benjamin frowned at her, then followed her up a flagstone walk* to the front porch. She found a key in her purse. When the door was opened she reached up to the wall just inside and turned on a hall light.

"Would you mind walking ahead of me to the sun porch?" she said.

"Can't you see now?"

"I feel funny about coming into a dark house," she said.

"But it's light in there now."

"Please?"

Benjamin waited a moment but then walked ahead of her down the hall and toward the rear* of the house.

"To your left," she said.

Benjamin walked to his left and down three steps leading to the sun porch.

closet *here* wardrobe **to back out** *G* rückwärts fahren **driveway** small path which leads to the garage **curb** *AE* = **kerb** *BE; G* Randstein **flagstone walk** path leading to the house made of flat squares of stone **rear** back

Mrs Robinson came in behind him and turned on a lamp beside a long couch against one of the walls.

"Thank you," she said.

"You're welcome."

"What do you drink," she said, "bourbon?"

Benjamin shook his head. "Look," he said. "I drove you home. I was glad to do it. But for God's sake I have some things on my mind. Can you understand that?"

She nodded.

"All right then."

"What do you drink," she said.

"What?"

"Benjamin, I'm sorry to be this way," she said. "But I don't want to be alone in this house."

"Why not."

"Please wait till my husband gets home."

"Lock the doors," Benjamin said. "I'll wait till you have all the doors locked."

"I want you to sit down till Mr Robinson comes back."

"But I want to be alone!" Benjamin said.

"Well I know you do," she said. "But I don't."

"Are you afraid to be alone in your own house?"

"Yes."

"Can't you just lock the doors?"

Mrs Robinson nodded at a chair behind him.

"When's he coming back," Benjamin said.

"I don't know."

Benjamin sat down in the chair. "I'll sit here till he gets back," he said. "Then I'll go. Good night."

"Don't you want some company?"

"No."

"A drink?"

"No."

Mrs Robinson turned and walked up the three stairs leading from the porch. Benjamin folded his hands in his lap and looked at his reflection in one of the large panels of glass enclosing the room. Several moments later music began playing in another part of the house. He turned and frowned at the doorway. Then Mrs Robinson walked back into the room carrying two drinks.

"Look. I said I didn't want any."

She handed it to him, then went to the side of the room and pulled a cord*.

cord thick string opening or closing the curtains

Two large curtains slid closed across the windows. Benjamin shook his head and looked at the drink. Mrs Robinson seated herself on a couch beside his chair. Then it was quiet.

"Are you always this much afraid of being alone?"

She nodded.

"You are."

"Yes."

"Well why can't you just lock the doors and go to bed."

"I'm very neurotic," she said.

Benjamin frowned at her a few moments, then tasted his drink and set it down on the floor.

"May I ask you a question?" Mrs Robinson said.

He nodded.

"What do you think of me."

"What?"

"What do you think of me."

He shook his head.

"You've known me nearly all your life," she said. "Haven't you formed any—"

"Look. This is kind of a strange conversation. Now I told my father I'd be right back."

"Don't you have any opinions at all?"

"No," he said. He glanced at his watch. "Look, I'm sure Mr Robinson will be here any minute. So please lock your doors and let me go."

"Benjamin?"

"What."

"Did you know I was an alcoholic?"

Benjamin shook his head. "Mrs Robinson," he said, "I don't want to talk about this."

"Did you know that?"

"No."

"You never suspected?"

"Mrs Robinson, this is none of my business*," Benjamin said, rising from the chair. "Now excuse me because I've got to go."

"You never suspected I was an alcoholic."

"Goodbye, Mrs Robinson."

"Sit down," she said.

"I'm leaving now."

this is none of my business this does not concern me; this has nothing to do with me

She stood and walked to where he was standing to put one of her hands on his shoulder. "Sit down," she said.

"I'm leaving, Mrs Robinson."

"Why."

"Because I want to be alone."

"My husband will probably be back quite late," she said.

Benjamin frowned at her.

"Mr Robinson probably won't be here for several hours."

Benjamin took a step backwards. "Oh my God," he said.

"What?"

"Oh no, Mrs Robinson. Oh no."

"What's wrong."

Benjamin looked at her a few moments longer, then turned around and walked to one of the curtains. "Mrs Robinson," he said, "you didn't—I mean you didn't expect ..."

"What?"

"I mean you—you didn't really think I would do something like that."

"Like what?"

"What do you think!" he said.

"Well I don't know."

"Come on, Mrs Robinson."

"What?"

"For God's sake, Mrs Robinson. Here we are. You've got me in your house. You put on music. You give me a drink. We've both been drinking already. Now you start opening up your personal life to me and tell me your husband won't be home for hours."

"So?"

"Mrs Robinson," he said, turning around, "you are trying to seduce* me."

She frowned at him.

"Aren't you."

She seated herself again on the couch.

"Aren't you?"

"Why no," she said, smiling. "I hadn't thought of it. I feel rather flattered that you ..."

Suddenly Benjamin put his hands up over his face. "Mrs Robinson?" he said. "Will you forgive me?"

"What?"

"Will you forgive me for what I just said?"

"It's all right."

to seduce *G* verführen

"It's not all right! That's the worst thing I've ever said! To anyone!"

"Sit down."

"Please forgive me. Because I like you. I don't think of you that way. But I'm mixed up!"

"All right," she said. "Now finish your drink."

Benjamin sat back down in his chair and lifted his drink up from the floor.

"Mrs Robinson, it makes me sick that I said that to you."

"I forgive you," she said.

"Can you? Can you ever forget that I said that?"

"We'll forget it right now," she said. "Finish your drink."

"What is wrong with me," Benjamin said. He took several large swallows from his drink and set it back on the floor.

"Benjamin?"

"What, Mrs Robinson."

She cleared her throat. "Have you ever seen Elaine's portrait?"

"Her portrait?"

"Yes."

Benjamin shook his head. "No."

"We had it done last Christmas. Would you like to see it?"

Benjamin nodded. "Very much."

"It's upstairs," she said, standing.

Benjamin followed her back to the front of the house and then up the thickly carpeted stairs to the second story. Mrs Robinson walked ahead of him along a hall and turned into a room. A moment later dim yellow light spread out the doorway and into the hall. Benjamin walked into the room.

The portrait was hanging by itself on one of the walls and the light was coming from a small tubular lamp* fixed at the top of the heavy gold frame. Benjamin looked at it, then nodded. "She's a very good looking girl," he said.

Mrs Robinson seated herself on the edge of a single bed in a corner of the room.

Benjamin folded his arms across his chest and stepped up closer to the portrait to study some of the detail of the face. "I didn't remember her as having brown eyes," he said. He stepped back again and tilted* his head slightly to the side. "She's really—she's really a beautiful girl."

"Benjamin?"

"Yes?"

She didn't answer. Benjamin turned to smile at her.

"Come here," she said quietly.

tubular lamp lamp which has the form of a tube; *G* Strahler **to tilt** to move sidewards

"What?"
"Will you come over here a minute?"
"Over there?"
She nodded.
"Sure," Benjamin said. He walked over to the bed. Mrs Robinson reached up to put one of her hands on his sleeve. Then she stood slowly until she was facing him.
"Benjamin?" she said.
"Yes?"
She turned around. "Will you unzip* my dress?"
Benjamin unfolded his arms suddenly and took a step backwards.
"I think I'll go to bed," she said.
"Oh," Benjamin said. "Well. Good night." He walked to the door.
"Won't you unzip the dress?"
"I'd rather not, Mrs Robinson."
She turned around again and frowned at him. "Do you still think I'm trying to …"
"No I don't. But I just feel a little funny."
"You still think I'm trying to seduce you."
"I don't," Benjamin said. "But I think I'd better get downstairs now."
"Benjamin," she said, smiling, "you've known me all your life."
"I know that. I know that. But I'm—"
"Come on," she said, turning her back to him. "It's hard for me to reach."
Benjamin waited a moment, then walked back to her. He reached for the zipper and pulled it down along her back. The dress split open.
"Thank you."
"Right," Benjamin said. He walked back to the doorway.
"What are you scared* of," she said, smiling at him again.
"I'm not scared, Mrs Robinson."
"Then why do you keep running away."
"Because you're going to bed," he said. "I don't think I should be up here."
"Haven't you ever seen anybody in a slip* before?" she said, letting the dress fall down around her and onto the floor.
"Yes I have," Benjamin said, glancing away from her and at the portrait of Elaine. "But I just—"
"You still think I'm trying to seduce you, don't you."
"No I do not!" He threw his hands down to his sides. "Now I told you I feel terrible about saying that. But I don't feel right up here."

to unzip *G* den Reißverschluß aufmachen **to be scared** to be afraid **slip** woman's undergarment, about the lenght of a dress

"Why not," she said.

"Why do you think, Mrs Robinson."

"Well I don't know," she said. "We're pretty good friends I think. I don't see why you should be embarrassed* to see me in a slip."

"Look," Benjamin said, pointing in back of him out the door. "What if—what if Mr Robinson walked in right now."

"What if he did," she said.

"Well it would look pretty funny, wouldn't it."

"Don't you think he trusts us together?"

"Of course he does. But he might get the wrong idea. Anyone might."

"I don't see why," she said. "I'm twice as old as you are. How could anyone think—"

"But they would! Don't you see?"

"Benjamin," she said, "I'm not trying to seduce you. I wish you'd—"

"I know that. But please, Mrs Robinson. This is difficult for me."

"Why is it?" she said.

"Because I am confused about things. I can't tell what I'm imagining. I can't tell what's real. I can't—"

"Would you like me to seduce you?"

"What?"

"Is that what you're trying to tell me?"

"I'm going home now. I apologize for what I said. I hope you can forget it. But I'm going home right now." He turned around and walked to the stairs and started down.

"Benjamin?" she called after him.

"What."

"Will you bring up my purse before you go?"

Benjamin shook his head.

"Please?" she said.

"I have to go now. I'm sorry."

Mrs Robinson walked out to the railing* holding her green dress across the front of her slip and looked down at Benjamin standing at the foot of the stairs. "I really don't want to put this on again," she said. "Won't you bring it up?"

"Where is it."

"On the sun porch."

Benjamin hurried through the hall and found the purse beside the couch on the sun porch. He returned with it to the foot of the stairs. "Mrs Robinson?"

"I'm in the bathroom," she called from upstairs.

to be embarrassed to feel uneasy/ashamed **railing** *G* Treppengeländer

"Well here's the purse."

"Could you bring it up?"

"Well I'll hand it to you. Come to the railing and I'll hand it up."

"Benjamin?" she called. "I'm getting pretty tired of this."

"What?"

"I am getting pretty tired of all this suspicion. Now if you won't do me a simple favor I don't know what."

Benjamin waited a moment, then carried the purse up to the top of the stairs. "I'm putting it on the top step," he said.

"For God's sake, Benjamin, will you stop acting this way and bring me the purse?"

He frowned down the hallway. A line of bright light was coming from under the bathroom door. Finally he walked slowly down the hall toward it. "Mrs Robinson?"

"Did you bring it up?"

"I did," he said. "I'm putting it here by the door."

"Won't you bring it in to me?"

"I'd rather not."

"All right," she said from the other side of the door. "Put it across the hall."

"Where?"

"Across the hall," she said. "In the room where we were."

"Oh," Benjamin said. "Right." He walked quickly back into the room where Elaine's portrait was and set the purse on the end of the bed. Then he turned around and was about to leave the room when Mrs Robinson stepped in through the door. She was naked.

"Oh God."

She smiled at him.

"Let me out," Benjamin said. He rushed toward the door but she closed it behind her and turned the lock under the handle.

"Don't be nervous," she said.

Benjamin turned around.

"Benjamin?"

"Get away from that door!"

"I want so say something first."

"Jesus Christ!" Benjamin put his hands up over his face.

"Benjamin, I want you to know I'm available* to you," she said. "If you won't sleep with me this time—"

"Oh my God."

to be available *G* zur Verfügung stehen

"If you won't sleep with me this time, Benjamin, I want you to know you can call me up any time you want and we'll make some kind of arrangement."
"Let me out!"
"Do you understand what I said?"
"Yes! Yes! Let me out!"
"Because I find you very attractive and any time—"
Suddenly there was the sound of a car passing along the driveway underneath the window.
Benjamin turned and leaped* at the door. He pushed Mrs Robinson aside, fumbled for* the lock then ran out the door and downstairs. He opened the front door of the house but then stepped back inside and hurried back onto the porch. He sat down with his drink and tried to catch his breath. The back door of the house slammed shut.
"Is that Ben's car in front?" Mr Robinson called.
"Yes sir!" Benjamin said, jumping up from the chair.
Mr Robinson came into the room.
"I drove—I drove your wife home. She wanted me to drive her home so I—so I drove her home."
"Swell," Mr Robinson said. "I appreciate it."
"She's upstairs. She wanted me to wait down here till you got home."
"Standing guard over* the old castle, are you."
"Yes sir."
"Here," Mr Robinson said, reaching for Benjamin's glass. "It looks like you need a refill."
"Oh no."
"What?"
"I've got to go."
Mr Robinson was frowning at him. "Is anything wrong?" he said. "You look a little shaken up."
"No," Benjamin said. "No, I'm just—I'm just—I'm just a little worried about my future. I'm a little upset about my future."
"Come on," Mr Robinson said, taking the glass. "Let's have a nightcap* together. I didn't get much of a chance to talk to you at the party."
Benjamin waited till Mr Robinson had left the room, then took several deep breaths. When he finished taking the deep breaths he put his hands in his pockets and walked quickly back and forth till Mr Robinson brought him his drink.
"Thank you very much, sir," he said as he took it.

to leap to jump **to fumble for** to reach for clumsily **to stand guard over** *G* Wache halten **nightcap** a drink before going to bed

"Not at all," Mr Robinson said. He carried his drink to the chair beside Benjamin's and sat. "Well," he said. "I guess I already said congratulations."

"Thank you."

Mr Robinson nodded and sipped at his drink. "Ben?" he said. "How old are you now."

"Twenty. I'll be twenty-one next week."

Again Mr Robinson nodded. "I guess you skipped a grade* or two back there in high school," he said. "I guess that's why you graduated so young."

"Yes sir."

Mr Robinson reached into his pocket for a package of cigarettes and held them out to Benjamin. He took one and put it in his mouth. "Ben?" Mr Robinson said, picking up a book of matches and lighting the cigarette for him. "That's a hell of a good age to be."

"Thank you."

Mr Robinson lit a cigarette for himself and dropped the match in an ash tray. "I wish I was that age again," he said.

Benjamin nodded.

"Because Ben?"

"What."

"You'll never be young again."

"I know."

"And I think maybe—I think maybe you're a little too worried about things right now."

"That's possible."

"You seem all wrapped up* about things," Mr Robinson said. "You don't seem to be—Ben, can I say something to you?"

"What."

"How long have we known each other now."

Benjamin shook his head.

"How long have you and I known each other. How long have your dad and I been partners."

"Quite a while."

"I've watched you grow up, Ben."

"Yes sir."

"In many ways I feel almost as though you were my own son."

"Thank you."

"So I hope you won't mind my giving you a friendly piece of advice."

"I'd like to hear it."

to skip a grade *G* ein Schuljahr überspringen **to be wrapped up about** to think too much about

"Ben?" Mr Robinson said, settling back in his chair and frowning up over Benjamin's head. "I know as sure as I'm sitting here that you're going to do great things someday."

"I hope you're right."

"Well I am right," he said. "That's something I just know. But Ben?"

"What."

"I think—" He dropped an ash from his cigarette into the ash tray. "I think you ought to be taking it a little easier right now than you seem to."

Benjamin nodded.

"Sow a few wild oats*," Mr Robinson said. "Take things as they come. Have a good time with the girls and so forth."

Benjamin glanced at the door.

"Because Ben, you're going to spend most of your life worrying. That's just the way it is, I'm afraid. But right now you're young. Don't start worrying yet, for God's sake."

"No."

"Before you know it you'll find a nice little girl and settle down and have a damn fine life. But until then I wish you'd try and make up a little for my mistakes by—"

Mrs Robinson, dressed again in the green dress and the gold pin she had worn to the party, stepped into the room.

"Don't get up," she said.

Benjamin sat back down in the chair. Mrs Robinson seated herself on the couch and picked up her unfinished drink from the floor.

"I was just telling Ben here he ought to sow a few wild oats," Mr Robinson said. "Have a good time while he can. You think that's sound advice?"

Mrs Robinson nodded.

"Yes I sure do," her husband said.

Benjamin finished his drink quickly and set it down on the table beside him.

"I've got to go," he said.

"Just hang on here, Ben," Mr Robinson said. "Wait'll I finish my drink, then I'm going to have you spin me around the block in that new car out front."

"Maybe he's tired," Mrs Robinson said.

"Tired, Ben?"

"Oh no. No." He picked up his glass and held it up to his mouth till the ice cubes clicked down against his teeth. Then he replaced it on the table.

"Do you want another?" Mrs Robinson said.

"What? No."

Sow a few wild oats *G* Tobe dich mal richtig aus

"Sure," Mr Robinson said. "You have yourself a few flings* this summer. I bet you're quite the ladies' man*."

"Oh no."

"What?" Mr Robinson said, grinning at him. "You look like the kind of guy that has to fight them off."

Benjamin reached for his glass.

"Are you sure you won't have another?" Mrs Robinson said.

"No. No."

Mr Robinson turned to his wife. "Doesn't he look to you like the kind of guy who has trouble keeping the ladies at a distance?"

"Yes he does."

"Oh say," Mr Robinson said. "When does Elaine get down from Berkeley*."

"Saturday," she said.

"Ben, I want you to give her a call."

"I will."

"Because I just know you two would hit it off real well*. She's a wonderful girl and I'm just awful sorry you two haven't got to know each other better over the years."

"I am too," Benjamin said. He watched Mr Robinson until he had taken the last swallow from his glass, then stood. "I'll take you around the block," he said.

"Great."

Benjamin walked ahead of Mr and Mrs Robinson through the hall and to the front door and opened it. Mrs Robinson stepped out onto the front porch after them.

"Benjamin?"

He put his hands in his pockets and walked down across the flagstone path without answering her.

"Benjamin?"

"What."

"Thank you for taking me home."

Benjamin nodded without turning around.

"I'll see you soon, I hope," she said.

"Hey Ben," Mr Robinson said, opening the door of the car and getting in. "What do you say we hit the freeway* with this thing and see what she does*."

You have yourself a few flings *G* Amüsier dich mal richtig **to be the ladies' man** *G* der Schwarm der Frauen sein **Berkeley** famous university in California (University of California) **to hit it off real well** to get on really well **to hit the freeway** to drive on the motorway **to see what she does** to see how good and fast the car is

2

During the next week Benjamin spent most of his time walking. On his twenty-first birthday he ate breakfast, then went out the front door, walked around the block, walked around the block again, then walked downtown. He walked back and forth along the main street till it was time to eat lunch, then went into a cafeteria. All during the afternoon he walked, sometimes stopping in a park or on a bus bench to rest a few minutes, but usually walking slowly past houses and stores, looking down at the sidewalk* ahead of him.

Late in the afternoon he returned to his own block and to his house. He walked up toward the front door but then stopped as he noticed several people sitting in the living room. He turned around and walked back toward the sidewalk but before he reached it the front door opened and his mother stepped out onto the porch.

"Ben?"

"What."

"Come on in."

"I'm going on a walk," Benjamin said.

Mrs Braddock hurried down toward the sidewalk to where he was standing. "It's your birthday," she said.

"I know that. I'm going for a walk on my birthday."

"Well the Arnolds came over from next door," she said. "I said you'd fix Peter and Louise some fruit juice as soon as you got back."

Benjamin took a deep breath, then turned around and walked with his mother slowly back to the house.

"I invited the Robinsons over," she said, "but Elaine had to stay up in Berkeley for summer school* and I—"

Benjamin had stopped and was staring at her. "Are they in there?" he said, pointing at the house.

"What?"

"Are Mr and Mrs Robinson in that house?"

"No."

"Are they coming?"

"No."

"Are you sure, Mother?"

"Of course I'm sure," she said. "Is anything wrong?"

"No," Benjamin said. He walked the rest of the way to the house and inside and to the living room.

sidewalk *AE* pavement **summer school** additional teaching in a college during the summer holidays

Mrs Arnold, seated in the middle of the sofa, began waving one of her hands back and forth through the air and singing the moment she saw him. "Happy birthday to you. Happy birthday to you. Happy birthday dear ..."

"Benjamin, it's good to see you," Mr Arnold said, standing up and shaking his hand.

Peter and Louise ran up to him and wrapped their arms around his legs.

Benjamin's father was sitting on one of the chairs beside the fireplace, a drink in his hand. "Go out and get the kids some fruit juice," he said. "Then come on back and we have a little surprise for you."

Benjamin walked slowly across the living room with Peter and Louise still hanging onto his legs and laughing. He pushed open the door of the kitchen and walked inside. "Get off my legs," he said when the door was closed.

They smiled up into his face.

"Get off my legs, I said!"

They released* his legs and walked slowly to one of the corners of the room.

Benjamin shook his head and opened the door of the refrigerator and looked inside. "What do you want," he said. "Grape juice or orange juice."

They stared at him from the corner without answering.

"Grape juice or orange juice!" Benjamin said, clenching* his fist.

"Grape juice."

"All right then." He reached into the refrigerator for a bottle of grape juice and filled two small glasses. Peter and Louise walked across the kitchen to take them.

"Thank you."

Benjamin poured himself a glass of grape juice and carried it back into the living room.

"Ben?" his father said, grinning at him. "I think you'll get a real big kick out of* your present this year."

Benjamin nodded and sat down on the sofa beside Mrs Arnold.

"We've been hearing all about it," Mrs Arnold said. "I can't wait to see it."

"Shall I bring it in now?" his father said.

"What."

"Your present."

Benjamin nodded and took a sip of the grape juice.

Mr Braddock stood and left the room. When he came back several moments later he was carrying a large square box wrapped in white paper. "Many happy returns*," he said, placing it on the rug at Benjamin's feet.

"I can't wait," Mrs Arnold said.

to release to let go **to clench one's fist** *G* die Hand zur Faust ballen **to get a kick out of** to be extremely amused **Many happy returns** *G* Herzlichen Glückwunsch

Benjamin looked at her a moment, then reached down to break two strips of Scotch tape* holding the paper together. Inside was a brown cardboard box. Mr Arnold crossed the room to stand over him and watch him open it. Benjamin pulled up the two flaps of the carton* and looked down into it.

"What is it," he said.

"Well pull her on up," his father said.

Inside the box was something made of black rubber that looked like several uninflated* inner tubes folded up on top of each other. Benjamin reached down and pulled it out.

"Now unfold it," his father said.

Benjamin held it up and let it unfold. It was a suit. There were two black arms and two legs and a zipper running up the front of it and a black hood*.

"What is it," Benjamin said. "Some kind of rubber suit?"

Mr Arnold laughed. "It's a diving-suit," he said.

"Oh," Benjamin said. He looked at it a moment longer, then nodded and began returning it to the box. "Thanks."

"You're not through yet," his father said, pulling it back up and holding it. "Keep digging."

"Isn't this exciting," Mrs Arnold said.

Peter and Louise came over to sit on the rug beside him and watch.

Benjamin reached down into the box and drew out a rubber mask with a glass plate in it, and two hoses* leading out from the side of it.

"That's your mask," his father said.

Peter Arnold took it from him to hold. Benjamin reached in again for a large silver cylinder with the words COMPRESSED AIR stenciled* on it in orange letters.

"That's your oxygen supply."

"I can see that," Benjamin said. He dropped the tank on the rug and reached into the box a final time and pulled up two black rubber fins*. He looked at them a moment, then dropped them back into the box and sat back on the couch. "Thanks," he said. He reached for his grape juice.

"Well now, let's have a show before it gets dark," Mr Braddock said.

"What?"

"I'll be right back," his father said. He turned around and hurried out of the room.

"What did he say?"

"I think he wants you to give us an exhibition out in the swimming pool," Mrs Braddock said.

Scotch tape *G* Tesafilm **flap of a carton** *G* aufklappbarer Teil einer Schachtel **uninflated** not blown up **hood** covering for the whole head *G* Kapuze **hose** tube **stenciled** printed (from a stencil) **fin** *G* Flosse

"Oh no," Benjamin said, straightening up on the couch.

Mr Braddock returned carrying a long metal spear and handed it to Benjamin.

"Listen," Benjamin said.

"Go on up and get your gear* on," his father said. "I'll set up some chairs out by the pool."

"Look," Benjamin said, shaking his head. "This is a great gift, but if you don't mind—"

"Let's go," Mr Braddock said. He began gathering up the equipment from the floor and handing it to Benjamin.

"Dad, it's just what I wanted and all that but I can't—"

"We want to be sure it's safe," his mother said.

"Safe? Sure it is. Look." He reached down into the floor of the box and pulled out a white slip of paper. "Here's the guarantee right here."

"Let's go," his father said, taking his arm and pulling him up from the couch.

"This is ludicrous*, Dad."

"Come on," Mr Arnold said, grinning at him. "Let's see a few underwater stunts*."

"Oh my God."

"Let's get to it," Mr Braddock said. He piled the equipment in Benjamin's arms and began pushing him toward the hall.

"Come on now, Dad."

His father left him standing in the hall and returned to the living room. Benjamin waited a moment, then walked back to the entrance of the room.

"Dad?"

"What're you still doing down here."

"Could I see you a minute, please?"

"Oh no. You get ready."

"Could I see you a minute in the hall, please!"

Mr Braddock walked back into the hall.

"Now I refuse to make a goddam ass* of myself in front of the Arnolds."

"Here we go," Mr Braddock said. He began pushing him towards the stairs.

"Goddammit, Dad!"

"Here we go," he said, pushing him up the stairs. "Happy birthday. Happy birthday."

"Dad I don't—"

"I'll give you three minutes to get it on," Mr Braddock said. He turned around and walked back into the living room. Benjamin stood a moment on the stairs

gear *G* Ausrüstung **ludicrous** ridiculous; grotesque **stunt** dangerous action, especially in films performed by stuntmen **to make a goddam ass of oneself** to make a complete fool of oneself with his arms wrapped around the equipment, then carried it up and into the bathroom. "Jesus Christ," he said, throwing it on the floor. He shook his head and kicked off his shoes. Then he removed the rest of his clothes and sat down on the toilet. He tugged* the rubber legs up around his own legs and forced his arms into the rubber arms and pulled up the zipper across his chest. He fixed the black rubber hood over his head and was about to return downstairs when he happened to glance out the bathroom window and into the back yard.

"Oh my God," he said.

The Arnolds and his mother were seated in metal chairs at one side of the pool. The two children were running back and forth on the grass. Standing at the other side of the pool were the Lewises, the other next-door neighbors and their teenaged daughter, and a man and a woman whom Benjamin had never seen before, standing beside them on the lawn holding drinks. At the rear of the yard the neighbors from in back were at the fence with their son. Benjamin pushed up the window.

"Say Dad?" he said.

Mr Braddock was pulling a final chair up beside the pool.

"Hey Dad! Could I see you a minute!"

Mr Braddock looked up at the window and grinned. "There he is, folks," he said, pointing at him. "Right up in the window there. He'll be right down." He held his hands up in front of him and began to applaud. The other guests gathered around the pool laughed and clapped. The Lewises' daughter turned to whisper something to her mother and her mother laughed and whispered something to their guests.

"Dad, for God's sake!"

"Hurry it up! Hurry it up! Folks," Mr Braddock said, "he's a little shy. This is his first public appearance so you'll have to—"

Benjamin slammed the window shut and stared down at the two fins and the air tank and the mask on the floor of the bathroom. Then he picked them up and carried them downstairs and out through the living room to the back. He stood looking out the door at the swimming pool and the guests until finally Mr Braddock rushed inside.

"Let's go."

"Does this amuse you?"

Mr Braddock leaned back out the door. "He's downstairs, folks! The suit's on! Give us half a minute!" He closed the door and stepped back inside. "I'll help you on with the mask," he said.

"Dad, this is sick."

to tug to pull hard

"Here." He took the mask and fitted it onto Benjamin's face. Then he strapped the air cylinder onto his back and connected it to the hoses running out the side of the mask. "Can you breathe all right?" he said. "Good." He got down on his knees and fitted the fins over Benjamin's feet, then stood up, grinned at him and walked back outside.

"Folks," he said. "Let's hear you bring him out! A big round of applause!" The guests began to applaud. "Here he comes! Here he comes!"

Benjamin stepped out the door and into the back yard. The neighbors continued to clap and laugh. Mr Lewis pulled a handkerchief out of his pocket to dry his eyes. The Arnold children began jumping up and down on the lawn and screaming and pointing at him. After several moments of applause Mr Braddock raised his hands. It was quiet.

"Now ladies and gentlemen? The boy is going to perform spectacular and amazing feats of skill and daring* under water."

Mr Arnold laughed. "Get your pennis ready, folks."

"Are you ready, boy?" Mr Braddock said. "All right then. On with the show!"

"On with the show!" the Arnold children yelled, jumping up and down. "On with the show! On with the show!" Mrs Arnold stood up and took their hands and then it was suddenly perfectly quiet in the yard.

Benjamin cleared his throat. He walked slowly toward the edge of the pool, keeping his chin down against his chest so he could see where he was going through the mask, but before he reached the water one of his flippers* got caught under his foot and he nearly pitched forward* onto his face. The children began to laugh again and leap up and down.

"Oh no," Mrs Arnold said. "That wasn't funny."

"Hey Ben," Mr Arnold called. "Be careful when you come up. You don't want to get the bends*."

Benjamin placed his foot down onto the top step at the shallow end of the pool, then walked slowly down the steps to the pool's floor.

"Wait a minute," his father said. He hurried to the edge of the pool with the spear. Benjamin stared at him a moment through the glass, then grabbed the spear away from him, turned around and began walking slowly down the slope of the pool toward the deep end. The water rose up around his black suit to the level of his chest. Then to his neck. Just as the water level was at his chin the flippers began scraping* against the bottom of the pool. He let all his breath out and tried to force himself under but the air tank kept him afloat. He began thrashing* with his arms but his head would not go under. The Arnold

feats of skill and daring *G* waghalsige Kunststücke **flipper** fin **to pitch forward** to fall forward **bends** *G* Taucherkrankheit **to scrape** to rub **to thrash** to move wildly children began to laugh. Finally he turned around and began moving slowly back up toward the shallow end. The neighbors in back began booing through the fence. By the time he reached the steps everyone in the yard was booing except for his father, who was standing at the head of the pool frowning at him.

Benjamin pulled the mask partially away from his face. "The show's over," he said quietly.

"What's wrong."

"He needs a weight!" Mr Arnold called. "That'll get him under. If you had a big rock it would do it."

"Right," Mr Braddock said. He straightened up. "Folks?" he said. "There will be a brief intermission*. Hang on to your seats." He hurried past the pool and through a gate into the rear part of the yard, where the incinerator* was.

Benjamin stood quietly at the shallow end of the pool resting the end of his spear on the pool's floor and staring through his mask at Peter Arnold. It was perfectly quiet. When Mr Braddock returned he was carrying a large piece of concrete* used to keep the lid* of the incinerator closed. Benjamin took it from him and walked slowly back toward the deep end. Some of the guests began laughing and applauding as his head went under and then it was perfectly quiet beneath the water as he walked gradually down to the very bottom of the pool. He stood a moment looking at a wall of the pool, then sat down. Finally he eased himself down onto his side and balanced the heavy piece of concrete on his hip. Then he turned his head to look up at the shiny silver surface of the pool above. "Dad?" he said quietly into his mask.

In the morning Benjamin got up earlier than usual. He dressed himself in a pair of khaki pants* and an old jacket he had bought in the East at an army surplus store*, and went downstairs. Mrs Braddock was in the kitchen. "You're up early," she said.

Benjamin walked past her and sat down at the table in front of his grapefruit. "I'm leaving home," he said.

"What?"

"I said I'm leaving home," he said, picking up his spoon. "I'm clearing out* after breakfast."

Mrs Braddock reached up to wipe her hands on a towel beside the sink. "You're going away?" she said.

"That's right."

intermission break; interval **incinerator** container for burning rubbish **concrete** *G* Beton **lid** top **khaki pants** trousers of a dull brownish or greenish yellow colour **army surplus store** shop where one can buy things that the army does not need any more, especially uniforms, boots, sleeping bags **to clear out** to leave

She frowned and walked across the room to sit down beside him at the table.

"You're taking a trip?" she said.

"That is right," Benjamin said. He dug into the grapefruit.

"Well where are you going," she said.

"I don't know."

"You don't know where you're going?"

"No."

She sat a moment looking at him. "I don't understand what you mean," she said.

"If you want the cliché," Benjamin said, looking up from his grapefruit, "I'm going on the road."

"What?"

"On the road. I believe that's the conventional terminology."

"Well Ben," his mother said.

"What."

"I still don't understand this. You aren't just planning to throw your things in the car and leave, I hope."

"No."

"Then what."

"I'm hitchhiking."

"What?"

"Mother, you haven't been on the road much, have you."

Mrs Braddock began shaking her head.

"Don't get excited, Mother. I'll be all right."

"You mean you're just going to pack your bag and go?"

"I'm not taking any luggage."

"What?"

"I'm taking what I have on."

"Are you serious?"

"Yes."

"Well how much money are you taking."

"Ten dollars."

"Oh," she said. "Then you won't be gone more than a day or two."

Benjamin raised a section of grapefruit to his mouth.

"How long will you be gone," his mother said.

"I don't know."

"More than a day or two?"

"Yes."

"But not more than a week."

"Look," Benjamin said. "Maybe five years, maybe ten. I don't know."

"What?"

Mr Braddock came into the kitchen carrying the morning newspaper. "You're up early," he said.

"Ben, tell your father. Because I know he won't let you do it."

"What's up," Mr Braddock said, sitting down at the table.

"I'm going on a trip."

"He's not taking the sports car. He's not taking any clothes. He has ten dollars in his pocket and he's—"

"Excuse me," Benjamin said. He reached for a bowl of sugar in the center of the table.

"What's all this about?" Mr Braddock said.

"I'm leaving after breakfast on a trip," Benjamin said, sprinkling sugar on his grapefruit. "I have no idea where I'm going. Maybe just around the country or the continent. Maybe if I can get papers I'll work around the world. So that's that."

"Well what's the point of it*."

"The point is I'm getting the hell out of here."

Mr Braddock frowned at him. "This doesn't sound too well thought out," he said.

Benjamin raised a sugared section of grapefruit to his mouth.

"You just plan to work around? Bum around*?"

"That's right."

"Meet all kinds of interesting people I suppose."

"That's right."

"Well Ben," his father said. "I don't see anything wrong with taking a little trip. But this is the wrong way to go about it."

"I don't think so."

"Listen," his father said. "How's this for an idea."

"I don't like it."

"How's this for an idea, Ben. Spend the summer picking out a graduate school in the East, then throw your things in the car and take a week or two driving back."

"No."

"What's wrong with that."

"Because I'm finished with schools, Dad." A section of grapefruit fell off his spoon and onto the table. "I never want to see another school again. I never want to see another educated person again in my life."

"Come on, Ben."

"Come on!" Benjamin said, standing up. "Now I have wasted twenty-one years of my life. As of yesterday*. And that is a hell of a lot to waste."

what's the point of it what's the use? **to bum around** to wander around without a (regular) job **as of yesterday** starting to count from yesterday

"Sit down."

"Dad," Benjamin said, "for twenty-one years I have been shuffling back and forth* between classrooms and libraries. Now you tell me what the hell it's got me."

"A damn fine education."

"Are you kidding me*?"

"No."

"You call me educated?"

"I do."

"Well I don't," Benjamin said, sitting down again. "Because if that's what it means to be educated then the hell with it."

"Ben?" his mother said. "What are you talking about."

"I am trying to tell you," Benjamin said, "I'm trying to tell you that I am through with all this."

"All what."

"All this!" he said, holding his arms out beside him. "I don't know what it is but I'm sick of it. I want something else."

"What do you want."

"I don't know."

"Well look, Ben."

"Do you know what I want," Benjamin said, tapping his finger against the table.

"What."

"Simple people. I want simple honest people that can't even read or write their own name. I want to spend the rest of my life with these people."

"Ben."

"Farmers," Benjamin said. "Truck drivers. Ordinary people who don't have big houses. Who don't have swimming pools."

"Ben, you're getting carried away."

"I'm not."

"Ben, you have a romantic idea of this."

"Real people, Dad. If you want the cliché, I am going out to spend the rest of my life with the real people of this world."

"Aren't we real?" Mrs Braddock said.

"It's trite* to talk about it," Benjamin said. "I know how I feel."

They finished breakfast quietly. When it was over, Mr Braddock pulled a checkbook out of his pocket and began making out a check*.

to shuffle back and forth *G* hin- und herlatschen **Are you kidding me?** Are you joking? **trite** useless; pointless **to make out a check** (cheque BE) *G* einen Scheck ausstellen

"Dad, look."
"I want you to take this," he said.
"I don't want it."
He signed it and tore it out of the book. "Here," he said.
"No."
"Take it."
"I won't."
Mr Braddock reached over to stuff it in the pocket of Benjamin's coat. Benjamin removed it, read the amount, then returned it to his pocket.
"Cash* it if you have to," his father said.
"I won't have to."
"All right. But Ben?"
"What."
"I don't know how long this is going to last. I have a feeling you'll be back here before you think you will."
"I won't."
"But if you feel you have to get out and rub elbows with* the real people for a while, then …"
Benjamin stood. "Goodbye," he said, holding out his hand.
His father shook it. "Call collect* if you get into any kind of trouble."
"Ben?" Mrs Braddock said. "Do you think you might be back by Saturday?"
"Mother."
"Because I invited the Robinsons over for dinner. It would be so much more fun if you were here."

to cash a check to exchange a check for money at a bank **to rub elbows with** to get into (close) contact with **collect (telephone) call** phone call to be paid for by the receiver

Part Two

3

The trip lasted just less than three weeks. It was late one night when Benjamin returned and both his parents were asleep. He tried the front door and found it locked. Then he tried the kitchen door at the side of the house and the door at the rear but both were locked. He attempted opening several windows but most of them were covered with screens and the ones without screens were locked. Finally he walked back around to the front porch and banged on the door until a light was turned on in his parents' bedroom. He waited till the light was turned on in the front hall. Then his father, wearing a bathrobe, pulled open the door.

"Ben," he said.

Benjamin walked past him and into the house.

"Well you're back."

"I'm back," Benjamin said. He walked to the foot of the stairs.

"Hey," Mr Braddock said, grinning at him, "it looks like you've got a little beard started there."

"It comes off tomorrow."

"Well," his father said. "How are you."

"Tired."

"You're all tired out."

"That's right."

"So how was the trip."

"Not too great," Benjamin said. He began slowly climbing up the stairs.

"Well Ben?"

Benjamin stopped and let his head sag* down between his shoulders. "Dad," he said. "I'm so tired I can't think."

"Well can't you tell me where you went?"

Benjamin knelt down on the stairs, then lay down on his side. "North," he said, closing his eyes.

"How far north."

"I don't know. Redding. One of those towns."

"Well that's where the big fire is," his father said. "You must have seen it."

Mrs Braddock, wearing her bathrobe and pushing some hair out of her face, appeared at the foot of the stairs. "Ben?" she said. "Is that you?"

to sag to sink

"Hello Mother," he said without opening his eyes.
"Are you all right?"
"Yes."
"Well how was the trip."
"Mother I have never been this tired in all my life."
"He got up to Redding, he thinks," Mr Braddock said. "One of those towns up there."
"Dad, I haven't slept in several days. I haven't eaten since yesterday and I'm about to drop over."
"You haven't eaten?" his mother said.
"No."
"I'll fix you something right away."
"Look," Benjamin said, raising his head up off the stair. "I'm so tired I can't even ..."
Mrs Braddock had already hurried out of the front hall and toward the kitchen.
"Come on in the living room a minute," Mr Braddock said. "You'll get to bed right after a little food."
Benjamin slid back down the stairs, stood and followed his father slowly into the living room. He dropped down onto the sofa.
"Well now," Mr Braddock said. "Let's have the report."
Benjamin's head fell back and he closed his eyes again.
"What about money. Did you cash my check?"
"No."
"Well what happened. Did you get some work?"
"Yes."
"What kind of work was it."
"Dad?"
"Come on, Ben," he said. "I'm interested in this."
Benjamin took a deep breath. "I fought a fire," he said.
"That big fire up there?" his father said. "You fought it?"
"That's right."
"Well that's right up there by Shasta. You must have been right up there in the Shasta country. That's beautiful country."
Benjamin nodded.
"How did they pay you on a deal* like that," his father said.
"Five an hour."
"Five dollars an hour?"
"That's right."

deal job; business

"They give you the equipment and you go in and try to put out the flames."

Benjamin nodded.

"Well what about the Indians. I was reading they transported some Indians up there from a tribe in Arizona. Professional fire fighters. Did you see some of them?"

"I saw some Indians. Yes."

Mr Braddock shook his head. "That is real exciting," he said. "What else happened."

Benjamin didn't answer.

"You didn't have any trouble getting rides*."

"No."

"Well tell me where you stayed."

"Hotels."

Mr Braddock nodded. "Maybe this trip wasn't such a bad idea after all," he said. "Did you have any other jobs besides the fire?"

"Yes."

"Well what were they."

"Dad, I washed dishes. I cleaned along the road. Now I am so tired I am going to be sick."

"Talk to a lot of interesting people, did you?"

"No."

"You didn't?"

"Dad, I talked to a lot of people. None of them were particularly interesting."

"Oh," his father said. "Did you talk to some of the Indians?"

"Yes Dad."

"They speak English, do they?"

"They try."

"Well what else did you—"

"Dad, the trip was a waste of time and I'd rather not talk about it."

"Oh?" his father said. "Why do you say that."

"It was a bore."

"Well it doesn't sound too boring if you were up there throwing water on that fire."

"It was a boring fire."

It was quiet for a few moments. "Can't you tell me a little more about it?"

"Dad—"

"Let's hear some of the people you bumped into*."

"You want to?"

"Sure," his father said. "What kind of people stopped to give you rides."

ride lift in a car **to bump into** to meet unexpectedly

"Queers*."

"What?"

"Queers usually stopped," he said. "I averaged* about five queers a day. One queer I had to slug* in the face and jump out of his car."

"Homosexuals?"

"Have you ever seen a queer Indian, Dad?"

"What?"

"Have you ever had a queer Indian approach you while you're trying to keep your clothes from burning up?"

Mr Braddock sat frowning at him from the chair. "Did that happen?" he said.

"Dad, for what it was worth I did the whole tour. I talked to farmers. I talked to—"

"What would you talk to them about."

"The farmers?"

"Yes."

"Their crops. What else do they know how to talk about."

"Who else did you talk to."

"I talked to tramps. I talked to drunks. I talked to whores*."

"Whores?"

"Yes Dad, I talked to whores. One of them swiped* my watch."

"A whore stole your wrist watch?"

"Yes."

"Not while you were talking to her."

"No."

Mr Braddock looked down at the rug. "Then you—then you spent the night with a whore."

"There were a few whores included in the tour, yes."

"More than one?"

"It grows on you*."

"How many then."

"I don't remember," Benjamin said, putting his hands up over his eyes. "There was one in a hotel. There was one at her house. There was one in the back of a bar."

"Is this true, Ben?"

"One in a field."

"A field?"

"A cow pasture, Dad. It was about three in the morning and there was ice in the grass and cows walking around us."

queer homosexual **to average** *here* to meet on an average **to slug** to give a strong blow; to hit **whore** prostitute **to swipe** to steal **It grows on you** you gradually like it

"Ben, this doesn't sound too good."

"It wasn't."

"I think you'd better go down and have yourself looked at."

"Dad, I'm tired."

"Is she the one who took your watch?"

"No. The one in the hotel took it."

"Ben," Mr Braddock said, shaking his head, "I don't know quite what to say. Where did you find these girls."

"Bars."

"They came right up to you?"

"Please let me sleep."

"I suppose you did quite a bit of drinking on the trip," Mr Braddock said.

Benjamin nodded.

"You did."

"Well it's not too likely I'd spend the night with a stinking whore in a field full of frozen manure* if I was stone cold sober, now is it."

"Good God, Benjamin."

Mrs Braddock returned to the room with a glass of milk and a plate with a sandwich on it. She set them down on the table in front of Benjamin.

"Now," she said. "Let's hear all about the trip."

Benjamin shook his head and reached for the sandwich.

"What did you do," his mother said.

"Not much."

"Well, can't you tell me about it?"

"Mother, I saw some pretty scenery and had a nice time and came home."

"And you're sure you're all right."

"Yes."

"Because you look awfully tired."

"Go on to bed," Mr Braddock said. "I want to talk to Ben a few minutes."

Mrs Braddock waited a moment, then walked out of the room.

"Ben, how do you feel about things now," his father said.

"What things."

"I mean are you—do you feel a little more ready to settle down and take life easy now?"

He nodded.

"You do."

"Yes."

"Well what are your plans. Do you think you'll go back to graduate school this fall?"

manure *G* Dung; Mist

"No."
Mr Braddock frowned. "Why not," he said.
"Dad, we've been through this."
"You still—you still feel the same way about teaching."
"That's right," Benjamin said. He reached for his milk.
"Well, do you have any plans?"
"I do."
"Can you tell me what they are?"
"I plan to take it easy," Benjamin said. "I plan to relax and take it easy."
"Good," his father said. "I'm glad to hear you say that. You plan to put in a little loafing time* around home."
"That's exactly right."
"Sure," his father said. "Rest up. Call up some girl who'd like to see you."
"I plan to."
"Good," Mr Braddock said. He sat in the chair across from him while Benjamin finished eating the sandwich and drank the glass of milk. Several times he glanced up at Benjamin, then back down at the floor. "Ben?" he said finally.
"What."
"You sound—you sound kind of disillusioned about things."
"I'm sorry."
"Are you disillusioned? Or are you just tired."
Benjamin stood up and wiped off his mouth with the back of his hand. "I don't know what I am, Dad, and I don't particularly care," he said. "Excuse me." He walked out of the room and up the stairs and went to bed.

Two days after he got home from the trip Benjamin decided to begin his affair with Mrs Robinson. He ate dinner with his parents in the evening, then went up to his room to take a shower and shave. When he had shined his best pair of shoes and dressed in a suit and tie he returned downstairs and told his parents he was going to a concert in Los Angeles. He showed them the article in the morning newspaper announcing the concert. Then he climbed into his car and drove to the Hotel Taft.
The Hotel Taft was on a hill in one of the better sections of town. A wide street curved up past large expensive homes until it neared the top of the hill, then there was an archway* over the street with a sign on the archway reading Taft Hotel and as it passed under the archway the street turned into the entranceway of the hotel. Benjamin drove slowly under the archway, then up the

loafing time time during which one does nothing **archway** an entrance with a curved top long driveway until he came to the building itself. He had to slow his car and wait in a line while other cars, most of them driven by chauffeurs, stopped by the entrance of the building for a doorman to open the door for their passengers. When Benjamin was beside the entrance an attendant* appeared at his car and pulled open the door.

"Thank you," Benjamin said as he climbed out.

Others the same age as Benjamin were walking across a broad pavilion* leading to the doors of the hotel. A few of the boys were wearing suits but most were wearing summer tuxedos* with black pants and white coats. A girl who had on a shiny white dress and a white orchid* on one of her wrists walked arm-in-arm with her escort up to the door and in. Benjamin followed. Just inside the door a man smiled at Benjamin and pointed across the lobby* of the hotel.

"Main ballroom," he said.

"What?"

"Are you with the Singleman party?"

"No," Benjamin said.

"I beg your pardon."

He nodded at the man, then walked into the large lobby, looking around him at the main desk and at the telephone booths against one wall and at the several elevators* standing open with their operators* in front of them. He walked slowly across the thick white carpet of the lobby to the door where the others had gone and for a long time stood looking into the ballroom. There were tables around the sides of the room covered with white tablecloths and in the center of each table was a small sign with a number on it. Some of the couples were wandering around the room looking for their tables and others were already seated talking together or leaning over the backs of their chairs to talk to someone at the next table. Just inside the door of the ballroom two women and a man were standing in a line. Each time a girl and her escort walked through the door the two women and the man smiled and shook their hands. Then the man reached into his pocket for a sheet of paper and told them where to sit.

"I'm Mrs Singleman," the woman closest to the door said to Benjamin after he had stood to watch several couples go in.

"Oh," Benjamin said. "Well I'm not—" She was holding out her hand to him. He looked at it a moment, then shook it. "I'm pleased to meet you," he said, "but I'm—"

attendant *here* person who looks after the guests of the hotel **pavilion** a light building which is attached to the hotel **tuxedo** *AE* dinner jacket *G* Smoking **orchid** exotic flower **lobby** entrance hall in a hotel **elevator** *AE* lift **operator** person who attends the elevator

"What is your name," she said.

"My name's Benjamin Braddock. But I'm—"

"Benjamin?" she said. "I'd like you to know my sister, Miss DeWitte."

Miss DeWitte, wearing a large purple corsage* on one of her breasts, stepped forward smiling and extended her hand.

"Well I'm glad to meet you," Benjamin said, shaking it, "but I'm afraid—"

"And that's Mr Singleman," Mrs Singleman said, nodding at her husband.

"How are you, Ben," Mr Singleman said, shaking his hand. "Let's see if we can't find you a table here."

"Well that's very kind of you," Benjamin said. "But I'm not with the party."

"What?"

"I'm—I'm here to meet a friend." He nodded and walked back past them and into the lobby.

Across from the ballroom was a bar with a sign over its door reading The Verandah Room. Benjamin walked across the lobby and under the sign and into the bar. He found an empty table in one of the corners of the room beside a large window that stretched across the entire length of the wall and overlooked the grounds of the hotel.

Although he seldom smoked Benjamin bought a package of cigarettes when he ordered his first drink and smoked several of them as he drank. He kept his face to the window, sometimes watching the reflection of people as they came in through the door of the bar and found tables, but usually looking through the glass at the lighted walks and the trees and the shrubbery* outside.

After several drinks he gave the waitress a tip and left the bar for the telephone booths in the lobby. He looked up the Robinsons' telephone number, memorized it and closed himself into a booth. For a long time he sat with the receiver in one hand and a coin in the other but without dropping it into the machine. Finally he returned the receiver to its hook and lighted another cigarette. He sat smoking it inside the closed booth and frowning down at one of the booth's walls. Then he ground it out under his foot and walked out of the booth and into the one beside it to call Mrs Robinson.

"I don't quite know how to put this," he said when she answered the phone.

"Benjamin?"

"I say I don't quite know how to put this," he said again, "but I've been thinking about that time after the party. After the graduation party."

"You have."

"Yes," he said. "And I wondered—I wondered if I could buy you a drink or something."

corsage a small bouquet of flowers **shrubbery** the bushes (shrubs) in the garden

A boy wearing a summer tuxedo closed himself into the booth beside Benjamin. Benjamin listened to him drop his coin into the telephone and dial.

"Shall I meet you somewhere?" Mrs Robinson said.

"Well," Benjamin said, "I don't know. I mean I hope you don't think I'm out of place or anything. Maybe I could—maybe I could buy you a drink and we could just talk. Maybe—"

"Where are you," she said.

"The Taft Hotel."

"Do you have a room there?"

"What?"

"Did you get a room?"

"Oh no," Benjamin said. "No. I mean—look, don't come if you—if you're busy. I don't want to—"

"Will you give me an hour?"

"What?"

"An hour?"

"Oh," Benjamin said. "Well. I mean don't feel you have to come if you don't—in fact maybe some other—"

"I'll be there in an hour," Mrs Robinson said. She hung up the phone.

Exactly an hour later she arrived. She had on a neat brown suit and white gloves and a small brown hat. Benjamin was sitting at the corner table looking out the window at the grounds of the hotel and didn't see her until she was standing directly across the table from him.

"Hello Benjamin."

"Oh," Benjamin said. He rose quickly from the chair, jarring* the table with his leg. "Hello. Hello."

"May I sit down?"

"Of course," Benjamin said. He hurried around the table and held the chair for her as she sat.

"Thank you."

Benjamin watched her remove the two white gloves and drop them into a handbag she had set on the floor. Then he cleared his throat and returned to his chair.

"How are you," Mrs Robinson said.

"Very well. Thank you." He looked down at a point in the center of the table.

It was quiet for several moments.

"May I have a drink?" Mrs Robinson said.

"A drink," he said. "Of course." He looked up for the waitress. She was on

to jar *here* to move with a harsh sound

the other side of the room taking an order. Benjamin whistled softly and motioned* to her but she turned and walked in the other direction. "She didn't see me," he said, rising from his chair and jarring the table. "I'll—"

Mrs Robinson reached across the table and rested her hand on his wrist. "There's time," she said.

Benjamin nodded and sat down. He kept his eyes on the waitress as she made her way to the bar and placed an order with the bartender*. As she turned around and waited for him to fill it Benjamin waved his arm through the air. "She saw me," he said.

"Good," Mrs Robinson said.

They drank quietly, Benjamin smoking cigarettes and looking out the window, sometimes drumming his fingers on the surface of the table.

"You've been away," Mrs Robinson said.

"What?"

"Weren't you away for a while?"

"Oh," Benjamin said. "The trip. I took a trip."

"Where did you go," Mrs Robinson said, taking a sip of her martini.

"Where did I go?"

"Yes."

"Where did I go," Benjamin said. "Oh. North. I went north."

"Was it fun?"

Benjamin nodded. "It was," he said. "Yes."

Mrs Robinson sat quietly a few moments, smiling across the table at him. "Darling?" she said.

"Yes?"

"You don't have to be so nervous, you know."

"Nervous," Benjamin said. "Well I am a bit nervous. I mean it's—it's pretty hard to be suave* when you're ..." He shook his head.

Mrs Robinson sat back in her chair and picked up her drink again. "Tell me about your trip," she said.

"Well," Benjamin said. "There's not much to tell."

"What did you do," she said.

"What did I do," Benjamin said. "Well I fought a fire."

"Oh?"

"Yes. The big forest fire up there. You might have—you might have read about it in the newspaper."

She nodded.

"It was quite exciting," Benjamin said. "It was quite exciting to be right up there in the middle of it. They had some Indians too."

to motion to make a signal **bartender** barman **to be suave** to be elegant/polite/agreeable

"Did you put it out?"

"What?"

"Did you get the fire out all right?"

"Oh," Benjamin said. "Well there were some others fighting it too. There were—yes. It was under control when I left."

"Good," she said.

Benjamin picked up his glass and quickly finished the drink. "Well," he said. "I'll buy you another."

Mrs Robinson held up her glass. It was still nearly full. "Oh," Benjamin said. He nodded.

"Benjamin?"

"What."

"Will you please try not to be so nervous?"

"I am trying!"

"All right," she said.

Benjamin shook his head and turned to look out the window again.

"Did you get us a room?" Mrs Robinson said.

"What?"

"Have you gotten us a room yet?"

"I haven't. No."

"Do you want to?"

"Well," Benjamin said. "I don't—I mean I could. Or we could just talk. We could have another drink and just talk. I'd be perfectly happy to—"

"Do you want me to get it?"

"You?" he said, looking up to her. "Oh no. No. I'll get it." He began nodding.

"Do you want to get it now?" she said.

"Now?"

"Yes."

"Well," he said. "I don't know."

"Why don't you get it."

"Why don't I get it now? Right now?"

"Why don't you."

"Well," Benjamin said. "I will then." He rose from the table. "I'll get it right now then." He walked a few steps away, stopped, then turned around and came back. "Mrs Robinson, I'm sorry to be so awkward about this but—"

"I know," she said.

Benjamin shook his head and walked across the Verandah Room. He stood for several moments in the doorway looking at the clerk behind the main desk, then finally pushed his hands down into his pockets and walked across the thick white carpet.

"Yes sir?" the clerk said.
"A room. I'd like a room, please."
"A single room or a double room," the clerk said.
"A single," Benjamin said. "Just for myself, please."
The clerk pushed a large book across the counter at him. "Will you sign the register*, please?" There was a pen on the counter beside the book. Benjamin picked it up and quickly wrote down his name. Then he stopped and continued to stare at the name he had written as the clerk slowly pulled the register back to his side.
"Is anything wrong, sir?"
"What? No. Nothing."
"Very good sir," the clerk said. "We have a single room on the fifth floor. Twelve dollars. Would that be suitable?"
"Yes," Benjamin said, nodding. "That would be suitable." He reached for his wallet.
"You can pay when you check out*, sir."
"Oh," Benjamin said. "Right. Excuse me."
The clerk's hand went under the counter and brought up a key. "Do you have any luggage?" he said.
"What?"
"Do you have any luggage?"
"Luggage," Benjamin said. "Yes. Yes I do."
"Where is it."
"What?"
"Where is your luggage."
"Well it's in the car," Benjamin said. He pointed across the lobby. "It's out there in the car."
"Very good sir," the clerk said. He held the key up in the air and looked around the lobby. "I'll have a porter bring it in."
"Oh no," Benjamin said.
"Sir?"
"I mean I'd—I'd rather not go to the trouble of bringing it all in. I just have a toothbrush. I can get it myself. If that's all right."
"Of course."
Benjamin reached for the key.
"I'll have a porter to show you the room."
"Oh," Benjamin said, withdrawing his hand. "Well actually I'd just as soon find it myself. I just have the toothbrush to carry up and I think I can handle it myself."

register list with the guests' names   **to check out** to leave the hotel

"Whatever you say, sir." The man handed him the key.

"Thank you."

Benjamin walked across the lobby and out through the front doors of the hotel. He watched the doorman open the doors of several cars and a taxi that drove up, then he turned around and went back inside. As he passed the clerk he stopped and patted one of the pockets of his coat. "Got it," he said.

"Sir?"

"The toothbrush. I got the toothbrush all right."

"Oh. Very good sir."

Benjamin nodded. "Well," he said. "I guess I'll stop in the bar a minute before going up."

"You do whatever you like, sir."

"Thank you."

Benjamin returned into the Verandah Room. Mrs Robinson looked up to smile at him when he came to the table.

"Well," Benjamin said. "I did it. I got it."

"You got us a room."

"Yes."

He reached into his pocket for the key. "It's on the fifth floor," he said, squinting* at the number of the key. "Five hundred and ten it is."

"Shall we go up?" Mrs Robinson said.

"Oh," Benjamin said, frowning. "Well I'm afraid there's a little problem."

"Oh?"

"I got a single."

Mrs Robinson nodded. "That's all right," she said.

"Well that's all right," Benjamin said. "But the man at the desk. The clerk. He seemed—he seemed like he might be a little suspicious."

"Oh," she said. "Well do you want to go up alone first?"

"I think I'd better," Benjamin said. "And also—also I was wondering if you could wait. Till he's talking to someone. So he—I mean I signed my own name by mistake and I—"

"I'll be careful," Mrs Robinson said.

"I know," Benjamin said. "But I don't know what their policy is here. I wouldn't—"

"Benjamin?"

"What."

"Will you try and relax please?"

"Well I'm trying," Benjamin said. "It's just that this clerk—he gave me a funny look."

to squint at *G* schielen auf

"I'll be up in ten minutes," Mrs Robinson said.

"Ten minutes," Benjamin said. "Right. I mean—right." He nodded and hurried away from the table.

In ten minutes Mrs Robinson knocked on the door of the room. Benjamin had just drawn two large curtains over the window. He hurried across the carpet and pulled open the door for her. They stood looking at each other for a moment, then Benjamin began nodding.

"I see—I see you found it all right," he said.

She smiled at him and walked into the room, looking at a television set in the corner, then at the bed. She removed the small round hat from the top of her head and set it down on a writing desk against one of the walls.

"Well," Benjamin said. He nodded but didn't say anything more.

Mrs Robinson walked slowly back to where he was standing. "Well?" she said, looking up into his face.

Benjamin waited a few moments, then brought one of his hands up to her shoulder. He bent his face down, cleared his throat, and kissed her. Then he lifted his face back up and nodded again. "Well," he said again, removing his hand from her shoulder.

Mrs Robinson returned to the writing table and looked down at her hat. "Benjamin?"

"Yes?"

"I'll get undressed now," she said, running one of her fingers around the edge of the hat. "Is that all right?"

"Sure," Benjamin said. "Fine. Do you—do you—"

"What?"

"I mean do you want me to just stand here?" he said. "I don't—I don't know what you want me to do."

"Why don't you watch," she said.

"Oh. Sure. Thank you."

He watched her unbutton the three buttons on the front of her suit, then reach up to unbutton the top button on her blouse. She smiled at him as she moved her hand slowly down the front of her blouse, then leaned for support on the writing table and reached down to remove her shoes.

"Will you bring me a hanger?" she said.

"What?"

She straightened up and frowned at him. "Benjamin, if you want another drink we'll go down and have one."

"Oh no," Benjamin said. "A hanger. I'll get a hanger." He hurried to the closet and opened its door. "A wood one?" he said.

"What?"

"Do you want a wood one?"

"A wood one would be fine," she said.

"Right," Benjamin said. He reached into the closet for a wooden hanger and carried it across the room to her.

"Thank you," she said, taking it.

"You're welcome," Benjamin said. He walked back to the door. He slid his hands into his pockets and watched her as she removed the jacket of her suit, then the blouse she was wearing and hung them on the hanger.

Suddenly Benjamin began shaking his head. He pulled his hands up out of his pockets and opened his mouth to say something but then closed it again. "Mrs Robin—?"

"What?"

"Nothing."

She frowned at him.

"Nothing," Benjamin said. "Nothing. Do you need another hanger."

"No," she said. She looked at him a moment longer, then pushed her skirt down around her legs, stepped out of it and folded it. "Would it be easier for you in the dark?" she said, draping the skirt through the hanger and over the wooden bar.

"No."

"You're sure."

"I'm sure. Yes."

"Hang this up, please?" she said. Benjamin walked across the room to take the hanger from her and carried it to the closet. When he had hung it up and turned around she had let a half-slip she was wearing drop to the floor and was stepping out of it. She slid a girdle* and the stocking fastened to it down around her legs and onto the floor. "Will you undo my bra*?" she said, turning around.

"Your—your—"

"Will you?"

Benjamin looked at her a moment longer, then suddenly began shaking his head. He rushed to one of the walls of the room. "No!" he said.

"What?"

"Mrs Robinson! Please! I can't!"

"What?"

"I cannot do this!"

Mrs Robinson watched him for a moment, then turned and walked slowly to the bed. She seated herself and moved back to sit with her back against the board at the head of the bed. She crossed her legs in front of her and reached

girdle women's undergarment to which the stockings are fastened **bra** a brassiere *G* Büstenhalter behind her back to unhook the bra. "You don't want to do it," she said.

"I want to but I can't!" he said to the wall. "Now I'm just—I'm sorry I called you up but I—"

"Benjamin?"

"I mean don't you see?" he said, turning around. "Don't you see that this is the worst thing I could possibly do? The very worst thing in the world?"

"Is it?"

He shook his head. "Now I feel awful about this," he said. "About having you come up here like this. But I—I just—Mrs Robinson, I like being with you. It's not that. I mean maybe we—maybe we could do something else together. Could we—could we go to a movie? Can I take you to a movie?"

She frowned at him. "Are you trying to be funny?" she said.

"No! No! But I don't know what to say! Because I've got you up here and I—"

"And you don't know what to do."

"Well I know I can't do this!"

"Why not."

"For God's sake why do you think, Mrs Robinson."

She shrugged*. "I suppose you don't find me particularly desirable," she said.

"Oh no," Benjamin said, taking a step toward the bed. "No. That has nothing to do with it."

"You don't have to—"

"Look," Benjamin said. "Mrs Robinson. I think—I think you're the most attractive woman of all my parents' friends. I mean that. I find you desirable. But I—For God's sake can you imagine my parents?" He held his arms up beside him.

"What?"

"Can you imagine what they'd say if they just saw us here in this room right now?"

"What would they say," she said.

"I have no idea, Mrs Robinson. But for God's sake. They've brought me up. They've made a good life for me. And I think they deserve better than this. I think they deserve a little better than jumping into bed with the partner's wife."

She nodded.

"So it's nothing to do with you. But I respect my parents. I appreciate what they've—"

"Benjamin?" she said, looking up at him.

"What."

to shrug *here* to raise the shoulders in order to express disappointment

"Would you think I was being forward* if I asked you a rather personal question?"

"Oh no," Benjamin said. "You can ask me anything you want. I'd be happy to—"

"Are you a virgin*?" she said.

"What?"

"You don't have to tell me if you don't want."

Benjamin frowned at her. "Am I a virgin," he said.

She nodded.

Benjamin continued to frown at her and finally she smiled. "All right," she said. "You don't have to tell me."

"Well what do you think," he said.

"I don't know," she said. "I guess you probably are."

"Come on," Benjamin said.

"Well aren't you?"

"Of course I'm not."

"It's nothing you should be ashamed of, Benjamin," she said, dropping her bra beside her on the bed.

"What?"

She folded her arms over her breasts and leaned her head back against the wall. "I mean I wish you'd just admit to me you're little bit frightened of being with a woman instead of ..."

"What?"

"I wish you'd just tell me you don't think you'd be able to go through with it rather than ..."

Benjamin shook his head. "Look," he said. "You're missing the point."

"I don't think so."

"Well you are," he said. "The point is that I come from a family where we trust each other."

Mrs Robinson brought her head up and smiled slightly. "Come on," she said.

"What?"

"Now look," she said. "I'm sure there isn't a man living who wasn't a little scared his first time."

"But it's not!"

"Benjamin there's no reason to be scared of me."

"Do you really believe that?" he said, taking another step toward the bed. "Do you really believe I've never done this thing before?"

to be forward to be frank and open but impolite at the same time **virgin** person without sexual experience

"Well," she said, "I think it's pretty obvious you haven't. You don't have the slightest idea what to do. You're nervous and awkward. You can't even—"
"Oh my God," Benjamin said.
"I mean just because you might be inadequate* in one way doesn't—"
"Inadequate?!"
She nodded, then it was quiet. Benjamin stared at her as she frowned down at one of her breasts. "Well," she said finally, straightening up and putting one foot down on the floor. "I guess I'd better be—"
"Stay on the bed," Benjamin said. He removed his coat quickly and dropped it on the floor. Then he began unbuttoning his shirt. He walked to the bed to sit down beside her, then reached behind her head to remove several bobby pins*. Mrs Robinson shook her head and her hair fell down around her shoulders. Benjamin finished taking off his shirt and dropped it on the floor. Then he put his arms around her and eased her down onto her back on the bed. He kissed her and kicked off his shoes at the same time. Mrs Robinson put her hands up at the sides of his head and then moved her fingernails up through his hair and finally wrapped both her arms around him and pressed him down against her until he could feel her breasts flattening underneath his chest and the muscles trembling in her arms. She pulled her mouth away from his and pushed it against his neck, then pushed one of her hands down between them to the buckle of his belt.
"Please," she said.
Benjamin raised his head up several inches to look at her face. Her eyes were closed and her mouth was partly open.
"Please," she said again.
Benjamin reached for the lamp on the table beside them. "Inadequate," he said, turning it off. "That's good. That's really pretty—"
"Please!"
He let her unbuckle his belt and push his pants down around his legs, then climbed on top of her and started the affair.

4

The date after which Benjamin was no longer eligible for the Frank Halpingham Education Award* fell sometime in mid-September. He celebrated the event quietly and by himself. When his parents had gone to bed he carried a bottle of

inadequate unable to fulfil her wishes **bobby pins** small pins women use to keep their hair in place **Frank Halpingham Education Award** (cp. page 7) bourbon* from the liquor cabinet out to the pool and drank it slowly and smoked cigarettes, grinding* the first ones out on the cement beside the pool and then flipping* the rest up in the air and watching them fall and sputter out* in the bright blue water. It was not till long after midnight that he tossed* the empty bottle into the pool, stood from his chair and walked slowly inside and upstairs to bed.

He spent most of his time at home. He got up late in the morning or early in the afternoon and dressed in his bathing suit. He usually ate breakfast by himself. Sometimes, if she wasn't shopping or reading in her room, his mother came into the kitchen to sit with him while he ate. After breakfast he went out to the pool. He had found an old rubber raft* in one of the cupboards of the garage which had not been used since before high school when the family had taken it on weekend trips to the beach. Benjamin inflated* it and although the rubber was cracked where it had been folded and stored, it still held air. After breakfast Benjamin usually kicked it into the water from the edge of the pool where he had left it the day before, then walked slowly down the steps of the shallow end. Sometimes he carried a can of beer down into the pool with him and sat on the raft while he drank it. Then he tossed the empty can off beside the pool and eased himself down onto the raft to float for the rest of the day. Sometimes he floated on his back with his hands folded across his stomach and sometimes he lay on his stomach with his arms hanging down into the water beside the raft. Unless it rained he floated all afternoon and right up until it was time for dinner, getting off the raft only once every hour or so to inflate it when he felt the water slowly rising up around his chest.

He ate dinner each evening with his parents. He put on a shirt and rolled up its sleeves around his elbows after his father insisted he wear more than his bathing suit to the table. After dinner, on the nights he didn't dress and drive to the Taft Hotel, he took a can of beer with him into the den* and watched television. During the early part of the evening he usually drank only beer as he watched television and then when it was later and his parents had gone to bed he usually poured himself a glassful of bourbon to drink as he watched the movies that came on after the shorter plays and comedy programs had ended. Sometimes, if his drink was still not finished, he sat a long time after the last movie was over watching one of the test patterns* or the photograph of an American flag that one of the channels always put on the screen after they had played the national anthem* and signed off the air. Once or twice he fell asleep

taking up again his old life

bourbon American whisky **to grind out** to put out **to flip up** to throw into the air **to sputter out** to go out with a hissing sound **to toss** to throw **rubber raft** air mattress **to inflate** to pump air into **den** a small room **test patterns** *G* Testbild **national anthem** *G* Nationalhymne

 drifting aimlessly

in his chair and woke up hours later just as it was beginning to get light outside to find that the can of beer or the drink he had been holding had fallen out of his hand and spilled* into his lap or across the rug. But usually the movies kept him awake. After a while he was able to calculate just how much to drink so that the moment the last movie ended he could set down his empty glass, turn off the set and go upstairs and be asleep almost the moment he slid in between the sheets of his bed.

One evening, an hour or so after dinner had been finished, Mr Braddock came into the den where Benjamin was watching television. Benjamin glanced at him, then back at the screen. Mr Braddock closed the door behind him and walked to the set to turn it off. Benjamin scowled at* him. Mr Braddock seated himself behind a desk in the room and looked for a long time without saying anything at an ash tray Benjamin had perched* on the arm of his chair.

"Ben?" he said finally, quietly. "What's happening."

"What's happening," Benjamin said, grinding out a cigarette.

"Yes."

"Well up until a minute ago I was watching TV."

Mr Braddock shook his head. "Ben, I don't know what to say to you."

"You don't."

"No."

"Well what's the problem then."

"You're asking *me* what the problem is?"

Benjamin shrugged and reached into the pocket of his shirt for a new cigarette. "I don't see that there is one," he said. "The only problem I see is that you came busting in* here and turned off a program."

"Ben," his father said, shaking his head. "Can't you talk to me? Can't you try and tell me what's wrong?"

"Look," Benjamin said. "Nothing's wrong at all. I mean you—you walk in here, you turn off the TV, you start wringing your hands and crying and asking me what's the problem. Just what in the hell do you want."

"Have you just lost all hope?"

"Oh my God," Benjamin said. He lit his cigarette and dropped the match into the ash tray.

"Well what is it then," Mr Braddock said, holding up his hands. "You sleep all day long. You drink and watch television all night. Sometimes you disappear after dinner and don't come home till the next day. And you're trying to tell me there's no problem? Ben, you're in a complete tailspin*."

"I'm in a complete tailspin."

to spill to run out accidentally **to scowl at** to look in an angry way **to perch** to place
to come busting in to rush/burst in **to be in a tailspin** to feel totally confused

"Ben," Mr Braddock said, "we are your parents."

"I'm aware of that."

"We want to know what you're doing. Ben, what do you do when you take off after dinner. Do you sit in bars? Do you go to the movies? Is there a girl you're meeting somewhere?"

"No."

"Well then what."

"I drive around."

"All the time?"

"That's right."

Mr Braddock shook his head. "That's rather hard to believe," he said.

"So don't believe it." Benjamin reached down for the can of beer on the rug beside his chair.

"And what are your plans. Do you have any plans at all?"

Benjamin swallowed some beer and returned the can to the rug. He wiped his mouth with the back of his hand. "Look," he said. "I'm perfectly content. All summer long you nagged at* me to have a good time. So now I'm having one. So why not leave well enough alone."

"This is what you call having a good time?"

"This is what I call having a ball*."

Benjamin finished his cigarette slowly. When he was done he ground it out in the ash tray and sat a few moments longer with his arms resting on the arms of the chair and staring ahead of him at the dark screen. Then he glanced up at his father. "Do I have your permission to turn on the television?"

"No."

"I don't."

"No."

Mr Braddock stood and walked to the window of the den. He looked out into the dark back yard. "I want to talk about this," he said.

"Dad, we've got nothing to say to each other."

"But we've got to, Ben."

"We don't."

"Ben I—I want to talk about values. Something."

"You want to talk about values," Benjamin said.

"Do you have any left?"

Benjamin frowned. "Do I have any values," he said. "Values. Values." He shook his head. "I can't think of any at the moment. No."

"How can you say that, son."

"Dad, I don't see any value in anything I've ever done and I don't see any

to nag at to criticize continually **to have a ball** to have a wonderful time value in anything I could possibly ever do. Now I think we've exhausted the topic*. How about some TV."

"You're twenty-one years old," his father said.

"Come on, Dad."

"You have a wonderful mind and you're a well-educated young man."

"Dad," Benjamin said, reaching into his shirt pocket for another cigarette, "let's not beat around the bush*. If you're trying to tell me you're throwing me out of the house why not come out with it."

"I'm not, Ben."

"Excuse me then. It sounded like you might be leading up to something of that nature."

"I'm leading up to this, Ben. There are certain things you seem completely unaware of."

"Such as."

"Well," Mr Braddock said, "such as a few economic facts of life if you want to put it that way."

"Economics."

"Yes."

"I think I'm aware of them."

"Are you?"

Benjamin nodded. "I seem to remember taking a course or two on that subject," he said.

"Well you don't seem to have gotten much out of it."

"As I recall," Benjamin said, lighting his cigarette, "I got the highest grade in the class."

Mr Braddock remained standing with his back to his son, looking out the window. "Well Ben," he said, "for all your intellectuality you don't—"

"I am not an intellectual!" Benjamin said. He dropped his match in the ash tray. "If you want to stand there and insult me I'd appreciate it if you'd stop short of that."

"For all your education, Ben, you seem rather naive about certain things. One of them is that someday you are going to have to earn a living."

"Am I?"

"Of course."

"Are you going broke* or something? You can't afford to feed me any more?"

Mr Braddock turned around to face him.

Benjamin stood. "Now look!" he said, waving his arm through the air. "I have

we've exhausted the topic there's nothing more to say on the subject **to beat around the bush** to approach a subject in an indirect way, without coming to the point **to go broke** to go bankrupt been a goddamn—a goddamn ivy-covered* status symbol around here for four years. And I think I'm entitled to—"

"What did you say?"

"What?"

"A status symbol? Is that what you said?"

Benjamin stared at him a moment, then looked down at the rug. "I didn't mean that," he said.

"Is that how you feel, Ben?"

"No."

"That your mother and I think of you as—"

"No!"

"Because—"

"Be quiet a minute. Now Dad? I appreciate everything you've done for me. I'm grateful for the education. But let's face it. It didn't work out. It wasn't worth a damn. Not one single damn thing was it worth."

Mr Braddock returned slowly to the desk and seated himself. "I don't know quite what to say," he said.

"I didn't mean that about the ivy-covered—"

"All right," he said. "But Ben?"

"What."

"Something has to be done. Maybe the education didn't work out, as you put it. Maybe it wasn't worth a damn. But you can't go on like this."

"I try not to bother anyone."

"Well that's hardly the point. Just the life you're leading is taking it out of both your mother and me. I'm afraid your mother's much more upset than she lets you know."

"I'm sorry about that."

"And let's be honest about this, Ben. Your mother and I are certainly as much to blame as you are for whatever is happening."

"No you aren't."

"Well we are. We've raised you. We've tried to instill* certain values into your thinking."

"Dad, I'm not blaming you."

"Well I'm blaming me then."

"Well you shouldn't."

"Ben," Mr Braddock said, "something is horribly wrong."

"Look Dad," Benjamin said. "This is getting kind of melodramatic. Why don't we—"

ivy-covered ironically refers to the Ivy League Colleges, such as Harvard and Yale **to instil** to put in drop by drop

"Just that?"

"What?"

"This is just melodrama to you?"

"Dad, look," he said. "The graduate comes home. He gets disillusioned. He gets bitter. He sits around home and goes to pot*. His parents wring their hands and blame his failings on themselves. I mean—yes." He nodded. "It has kind of a hearts and flowers ring to it*."

Mr Braddock was about to say something more when he was interrupted by a knock on the door. Mrs Braddock opened it and looked into the room.

"Mr and Mrs Robinson are here," she said. "Will you come out and say hello?"

Benjamin took a step backward toward the other door. "I'll be in my room," he said.

"Ben?"

"Mother, I don't feel too well."

His father was frowning at him from the desk. "Ben?" he said.

"What."

"What's going on."

"I don't know," Benjamin said. "I get these cramps sometimes after dinner. It helps if I lie down."

Still frowning at him, his father rose from his chair. Benjamin glanced up at them a moment, then down at the floor. "There," he said. "There. It's better." He nodded.

"Will you come out and say hello to the Robinsons?"

"Sure. I'd like to."

Mrs Robinson was standing with her back to the fireplace, wearing the same brown suit she had worn the first night Benjamin had met her at the hotel.

"Hi," Benjamin said.

"How are you."

"Fine thank you."

"Looks like you've been in for a swim," Mr Robinson said, holding out his hand.

"Yes sir," Benjamin said, shaking it. "This afternoon. I guess—I guess I haven't gotten around to changing yet."

"Well," Mr Robinson said. "Have a seat. I haven't seen you for a while."

Benjamin sat down on the sofa. Mr Robinson sat beside him.

"What're you up to."

"Sir?"

to go to pot to go to ruin **It has kind of a hearts and flowers ring to it** it sounds sort of sentimental and romantic

"What're you doing with yourself these days."

"Oh," Benjamin said. "Not too much. Taking it easy."

Mr Robinson nodded. "That's what I'd do if I could," he said. "Nothing wrong with that."

"Yes sir. Thank you."

"So what are your plans," Mr Robinson said.

"Indefinite," Benjamin said.

"I guess you've pretty well given up this teaching idea you had."

"Don't speak too soon," Mrs Braddock said.

"What?"

"I still think Ben's going to be a teacher someday."

"I might at that," Benjamin said. "I guess I can't—I guess it's pretty hard to say at this stage of the game."

"Sure it is," Mr Robinson said. "You take it easy. How's the girl situation."

"What?"

"Have you dug up any of those old girls you used to go to high school with?"

Benjamin shook his head. "I haven't been doing much dating," he said.

"Well what's wrong with you."

"What?"

"Come on," Mr Robinson said, winking at his mother. "You can't tell me you don't have somebody stashed away*."

"Oh no. No. No."

"Where's the old college spirit."

"No. I mean I don't—I don't—"

"Excuse me," Mrs Robinson said. "I'll find a glass of water." She left the room.

"Ben, you go help her," Mrs Braddock said.

Benjamin stood up and hurried out to the kitchen with Mrs Robinson. "The glasses are up here," he said. He reached up and handed her one.

"Benjamin?"

"Be quiet," he said.

"Benjamin, I think you'd better go up to your room or something."

Benjamin shook his head and walked quickly out of the kitchen and back into the living room. Mrs Robinson filled her glass and followed him.

"Hey Ben," Mr Robinson said.

"Yes?"

"Come on back and sit down a minute."

Benjamin returned to the sofa.

stashed away put away or hidden

"Elaine's coming down for a few days at Thanksgiving*. I want you to call her up this time."
"I will."
"I mean it."
"I know," Benjamin said. "I know you do."
"Because I just think you two would hit it off real well together."
Benjamin nodded. "When—I mean when does she get down," he said.
"I'm not sure of the exact date," Mr Robinson said. "I'll let your father know when I find out."
For a long time it was quiet. Benjamin sat looking down at the rug. Once he glanced up at his mother, who was sitting in her chair watching him, then he looked for a moment at his father's shoes and quickly back at the rug in front of him. His mother cleared her throat. Mr Robinson moved slightly on the couch beside him. Then it was perfectly quiet again.
"What—what's wrong?" Benjamin said.
"I know what I wanted to ask you," Mrs Robinson said, walking across the room. "Where did you find this lamp?"
Everyone turned to watch her bend over and look at a lamp on the table in the corner of the room.
"Where did that come from," Mrs Braddock said. "Wasn't that given to us?"
Mr Braddock nodded. "It was a gift," he said. "We've had it for years."
"I was looking for one this size last week," she said. "But I don't think they make them any more."
"I'll keep my eye open," Mrs Braddock said.
"Would you?"
"Surely."
Mrs Robinson smiled at her, then turned to her husband and raised her eyebrows. "We really should run," she said.

Later in the evening Benjamin was standing in his room at the window when his mother opened the door and stepped inside. "Can I talk to you a minute?" she said.
"What? Sure."
She closed the door behind her. "Benjamin?" she said. "Can I ask you what's on your mind?"
He frowned at her.
"There's something on your mind," she said. "Can you tell me what it is?"
He shrugged his shoulders. "I don't know," he said.

Thanksgiving a national holiday celebrated on the fourth Thursday in November, on which God is thanked for the crops

"Is it something to do with the Robinsons?"

"What?"

"You seemed—you seemed awfully uncomfortable downstairs with the Robinsons."

Benjamin nodded. "I was," he said.

"Well is—is something wrong?"

He nodded again and walked to the window. "Mother," he said, "I feel guilty."

"What?"

"I feel guilty sitting around home like this. I'm afraid your friends think I'm just a bum*."

"Oh no, Ben."

"Well I get that feeling," Benjamin said. "I got it the other night when the Terhunes were here. Then I got it tonight when the Robinsons came over."

"Ben, they think the world of you."

"They think I should be out working. They think I should be at school."

"Oh no, Ben," she said. She walked across the room to him and took his hand. He pulled it away and shook his head.

"I feel worthless, Mother. I feel rotten about what I'm doing."

"You'll get over this, Ben," she said. "It's just a stage you're in. You'll get over it."

"Well I hope so."

"You will," she said. "So don't worry about it. Our friends think you're one of the finest people they know."

Benjamin nodded. His mother turned around and walked back toward the door, then stopped. "Benjamin?"

"What."

"I'm going to ask you something but you don't have to tell me if you don't want."

"What," he said.

"Well I'm going to ask you what you do when you go off at night."

"When I go off?"

She nodded.

Benjamin frowned down at the rug and began shaking his head.

"You don't have to tell me if you don't want."

"No, I do," he said. "I want to tell you."

It was quiet for several moments.

"I drive around," he said.

bum a worthless person

"What else."

"Nothing else."

"Well you don't drive around from midnight till noon the next day, Benjamin."

"Oh no."

"Then what do you do. Do you meet someone?"

"Meet someone?"

She nodded.

"Why did you say that."

"Well this is your business, Benjamin," she said, turning back toward the door. "If you—"

"No wait. Wait."

She stopped.

"I don't meet anyone, Mother, but why did you say that."

She shook her head. "Because I can't imagine what else you'd do."

"But what do you mean by 'meet someone'."

"Let's forget it."

"No."

"Benjamin, I'm not going to pry* into your affairs," she said, "but I'd rather you didn't say anything at all than be dishonest."

"What?"

"Good night. Benjamin."

"Well wait."

She frowned at him.

"You think I'm being dishonest?"

She nodded.

"Well why do you—why do you think that."

"Because I know you don't drive around for twelve hours."

"Oh," Benjamin said. "Well I don't. Shall I tell you what I do?"

"Not if you don't want."

"I do."

"But I don't want you to make up something."

"I'm not," Benjamin said. "But I'm—I'm not very proud of what I do. I usually get kind of drunk. I usually drive over to Los Angeles and go to some bars and get kind of drunk. Then I take a hotel room. So I won't have to drive home on the freeway. I mean it kind of scares me to drive home after—"

"Good night, Benjamin."

"What?"

"I'll see you tomorrow."

to pry into to stick one's nose into

"Well Mother?"

"What."

"You believe me, don't you."

"No."

"You don't?"

She shook her head.

"But I want you to," he said. "Please. Please will you believe me!"

"Good night," she said.

As soon as she had left the room Benjamin sat down at his desk and pulled out a sheet of stationery* to write a letter to Mrs Robinson.

Dear Mrs Robinson,

I cannot go on seeing you. It is ruining me and it is ruining my parents and I am a nervous wreck. My life is going quickly down the drain* and right now at this moment I have got to do something. I don't know what. I am in a complete tailspin. I am thoroughly despicable in everything I am doing with you. Please burn this letter as soon as you have read it.

I am going to teach. I will see if they might possibly give me the award back and if not I will either work my way through graduate school somehow or accept a position at one of the colleges that made offers while I was still at school. That is the only possible choice I have other than being a filthy degenerate* all my life. I hope you will understand that this decision in no way reflects upon* yourself insofar as your desirability etc. are concerned but I can't live with myself any longer as I am. When you and your husband were here tonight it was all I could do to keep from screaming and running out of the room. I don't know why I should feel that way because I do not think what we are doing is of much consequence but for some reason it is making a nervous wreck of me which is something I don't particularly want to be the rest of my life.

The door of Benjamin's room opened suddenly. His hand froze on the page.

"Ben?" his father said.

Benjamin looked quickly around the desk and then slid the stationery box over the letter and stood.

"Ben," his father said, "your mother tells me you're a little worried about what our friends think of you."

"Oh," Benjamin said. "Well. I hate—I hate for them to think I'm just loafing around*."

"Well Ben, what's happening is a problem. It's a terribly serious problem. But don't worry about our friends because they know you're a wonderful person."

stationery writing paper **My life is going quickly down the drain** my life is being wasted **filthy degenerate** a useless bum **in no way reflects upon** *here* has nothing to do with **I hate for them to think I'm just loafing around** I don't want them to think that I'm wasting my time

Benjamin nodded. "Well I feel—I feel a little uncomfortable with them sometimes."
"It's Mrs Robinson, isn't it."
"What?"
"Mrs Robinson makes you feel a little uncomfortable, doesn't she."
"Well no," Benjamin said, suddenly shaking his head. "She's—I mean I don't—"
"Ben, I've known that woman for nearly twenty years and I still don't know her."
"What?"
"She's a funny one, Ben."
"Oh," Benjamin said.
"There's something about her that makes anybody feel uncomfortable. I don't know what. But don't let it—don't let it throw* you." Mr Braddock folded his arms across his chest. "Ben," he said. "I'm afraid they're a pretty miserable couple."
"They are?"
"I think so," he said. "I think she gives him a pretty hard time. I've never spoken to him about it but I think he's pretty disappointed with her."
"Oh," Benjamin said. He sat back down in the chair.
"You won't let this go beyond you and me."
"Oh no."
"But she's—she's really not much of a person. She never says much. She never makes any effort socially or any other way." He shook his head. "I'd be interested to know how they ever got together in the first place."
"Well," Benjamin said. "She's—I think she's fairly good looking."
"She's damn attractive," his father said. He stood looking down at the rug a few moments. "But she's not honest, Ben."
"She's not."
"I don't think so. I think she's devious*. I don't think she was ever taught the difference between right and wrong the way you and I were. It's just a feeling I get about her. I couldn't tell you why." He looked up to smile. "So," he said, "don't let her throw you."
"I won't."
"What are you doing there?"
"What?"
"Writing a letter?"
"Oh yes. Yes I am. This boy I graduated with. We were going to keep in touch but we never did."

to throw *here* to confuse **devious** not straightforward

"Good," his father said, grinning at him. "Keep up the old contacts. You never know when they'll come in handy*." He turned and walked out the door.

Benjamin waited till he was downstairs, then closed the door and locked it. He returned to his desk and slid the stationery box off the letter and continued.

I don't know if you were ever taught the difference between right and wrong or not, but since I was, I feel a certain obligation to it and cannot continue in as devious a fashion as I have been. Since we never exactly lose ourselves in conversation I'm not sure how you feel about things but obviously what we are doing can only lead to some kind of disaster if we go on, so I feel, and hope you do, that this is a good place to stop. Please don't think I haven't enjoyed having an affair with an "older woman" as I have not only enjoyed it but consider it a worth-while part of my general education. But it will be much better, I know, to remember it as it has been rather than as something it might become.

Best wishes,
Benjamin

"I got your note," Mrs Robinson said, several evenings later over their drink in the Verandah Room.

"The note," Benjamin said. "I'm afraid I got a little carried away* there for a moment."

"Devious?" she said.

"What?"

"Do you really think I'm devious?"

"I said I got carried away. Now let's forget about it."

The affair continued on into the fall. At first Mrs Robinson had sent Benjamin a note in the mail whenever she wanted to see him and he had met her in the Verandah Room the next evening near midnight. During the first month the notes had arrived not more than once a week. Then they began to arrive more frequently and finally Benjamin asked her not to send them because his mother usually took in the mail before he got up and had asked him several times who was sending them. Instead it was arranged that Benjamin would call Mrs Robinson each afternoon and she would tell him over the phone if she could be at the hotel that night. One week he met her five nights in a row.

On the days that he met her Benjamin would eat dinner with his parents as usual, watch television until nearly midnight, then dress in his suit and drive to the hotel. At the hotel he would buy Mrs Robinson a martini, then take a room for them. In the beginning he had gone up ahead to wait for her but after the first few weeks he waved at her from the entrance of the bar when he had gotten the room and they rode up together in the elevator. When they got in

to come in handy to be useful **to get carried away** to get over-excited through emotions the room Benjamin always called down to the desk and left word that they were to call up to his room before dawn. When the call came Mrs Robinson would get up and dress and drive home to fix breakfast for Mr Robinson. Benjamin usually would not wake up till late in the morning. Then he would take a shower, dress and pay for the room on his way out of the hotel.

They seldom spoke to each other after the first several times. Usually they sat at a table next to the window in the Verandah Room looking out the window at the grounds of the hotel.

"Mrs Robinson?" Benjamin said one night when the drinks had been brought to the table.

"What."

"I don't want to interrupt your thoughts, but do you think we might do a little talking?"

"What?"

"I say we don't seem to have very lively conversations, do we."

"No we don't," she said.

Benjamin nodded and turned to look at a palm tree outside in the grounds. He finished his drink without saying anything more, then stood. "I'll get the room," he said. He walked into the lobby and to the desk.

"Give me a twelve-dollar single," he said.

"Yes sir," the clerk said. He pushed the register across the desk and Benjamin signed. "Any luggage tonight, Mr Gladstone?" he said.

Benjamin shook his head and walked back into the Verandah Room and to the table and dangled* the key in front of Mrs Robinson's face. "Let's go," he said.

They rode up in the elevator without talking and walked quietly down the hall and Benjamin opened the door and they walked in and shut it, still without saying anything. Mrs Robinson removed her coat and dropped it on one of the chairs. Then she smiled at Benjamin and walked across the room to him and reached up to untie the knot of his tie.

"Wait a minute," Benjamin said. He pushed her hand away. "Sit down a minute," he said.

Mrs Robinson raised her eyebrows.

"Will you please sit down a minute," Benjamin said, pointing at the bed.

Mrs Robinson waited a moment, then turned around and walked to the bed. She seated herself on the end of it and reached down to remove one of her shoes.

"No," Benjamin said.

"What?"

to dangle to swing loosely

"Will you leave the shoe on for a minute. Please."

She nodded and straightened up.

"Now," Benjamin said. "Do you—do you think we could just say a few words to each other first this time?"

"If you want."

"Good," Benjamin said. He pushed her coat to the side of the chair and seated himself. Then for a long time he sat looking down at the rug in front of him. It was perfectly quiet. He glanced up at her, then back down at the carpet.

"I mean are we dead or something?" he said.

"Well I just don't think we have much to say to each other."

"But why not!"

She shrugged her shoulders.

"I mean we're not stupid people, are we?"

"I don't know."

"Well we aren't," he said. "But all we ever do is come up here and throw off the clothes and leap into bed together."

"Are you tired of it?"

"I'm not. No. But do you think we could liven it up* with a few words now and then?"

She didn't answer him.

"Look," Benjamin said, standing up. "Now there is something wrong with two human beings who know each other as intimately as we do who can't even speak together."

"Well what do you want to talk about, darling."

"Anything," he said, shaking his head. "Anything at all."

"Do you want to tell me about some of your college experiences?"

"Oh my God."

"Well?"

"Mrs Robinson. If that's the best we can do let's just get the goddamn clothes off and—"

She reached down for her shoes.

"Leave it on!" Benjamin said. "Now we are going to do this thing. We are going to have a conversation. Think of another topic."

"How about art."

"Art," Benjamin said. He nodded. "That's a good subject. You start it off."

"You start it off," she said. "I don't know anything about it."

"Oh."

"Don't you?"

"Yes I do," Benjamin said. "I know quite a bit about it."

to liven up to make more lively

"Go ahead then."
Benjamin nodded. "Art," he said. "Well what do you want to know about it."
She shrugged.
"Are you interested more in modern art or more in classical art."
"Neither," she said.
"You're not interested in art?"
"No."
"Then why do you want to talk about it."
"I don't."
Benjamin nodded and looked back down at the rug.
"Can I take off my clothes now?"
"No. Think of another topic."
Mrs Robinson looked up at the ceiling a moment. "Why don't you tell me what you did today," she said.
Benjamin stood up and walked to one of the curtains. "Mrs Robinson?" he said. "This is pathetic*."
"You don't want to tell me about your day?"
"My day," Benjamin said.
"Let's go to bed."
"I got up."
"What?"
"I am telling you about my day, Mrs Robinson."
"Oh."
"I got up in the morning. About twelve. I ate breakfast. After breakfast I had some beers. After the beers I went out to the pool. I blew air in the raft. I put the raft on the water. I got in the water myself. I floated on the raft."
"What are you talking about," Mrs Robinson said.
"I have this raft I float on in the afternoons," he said.
"Oh."
"Then I ate dinner. After dinner I watched two quiz shows. Then I watched half a movie. Then I came here. Now. Tell me about your day."
"Do you want me to?"
"Yes I do."
"I got up," she said.
Benjamin began shaking his head.
"Do you want to hear it or not?"
"Yes," Benjamin said. "But you might try and spice it up* with a little originality."

pathetic causing pity   **to spice up** to make more interesting

"I got up," Mrs Robinson said again. "I ate breakfast and went shopping. During the afternoon I read a novel."

"What one."

"What?"

"What novel did you read."

"I don't remember."

Benjamin nodded.

"Then I fixed dinner for my husband and waited until—"

"There!" Benjamin said, whirling around and pointing at her.

"What?"

"Your husband! Mr Robinson! There's something we could have a conversation about."

"Him?"

"I mean everything," Benjamin said. "I don't know anything about how you—how you work this. I don't know how you get out of the house at night. I don't know the risk involved."

"There isn't any," she said.

"There's no risk?"

She shook her head.

"But how do you work it. How do you get out of the house."

"I walk out."

"You walk right out the door?"

She nodded.

"But your husband. What do you say to him."

"He's asleep."

"Always?"

"Benjamin, this isn't a very interesting topic."

"Please," Benjamin said. "Now tell me. How do you know he won't wake up sometime and follow you."

"Because he takes sleeping pills."

"But what if he forgets."

"What?"

"What if he forgets to take them. What if they don't work one night."

"He takes three sleeping pills every night at ten o'clock. Now why don't we—"

"No wait," Benjamin said. "I want to know these things. I mean I can think about them. At ten o'clock I can think about Mr Robinson taking his three pills." He cleared his throat. "So," he said. "He takes the pills. But what about the noise from the car. What if—"

"The driveway's on my side of the house."

"We're talking," Benjamin said, smiling suddenly.

“What?”

“We’re talking, Mrs Robinson. We’re talking!”

“Calm down, Benjamin.”

“Now let’s keep going here,” he said, seating himself again in the chair. “‘Can I undress and talk at the same time?’”

“Right.”

“Thank you.”

“Now,” Benjamin said. “You say the driveway’s on your side of the house.”

She nodded and began unbuttoning her blouse.

“So I guess you don’t sleep in the same room.”

“We don’t.”

“So you don’t ... I mean I don’t like to seem like I’m prying but I guess you don’t sleep together or anything.”

“No we don’t,” she said, unbuttoning the final button.

“Well how long has this been going on.”

“What.”

“That you’ve been sleeping in different rooms. Different beds.”

Mrs Robinson looked up at the ceiling a moment. “About five years,” she said.

“Oh no.”

“What?”

“Are you kidding me?”

“No.”

“You have not slept with your husband for five years?”

“Now and then,” she said, removing the blouse. “He gets drunk a few times a year.”

“How many times a year.”

“On New Year’s Eve,” she said. “Sometimes on his birthday.”

Benjamin shook his head. “Man, is this interesting,” he said.

“Is it?”

“So you don’t love him. You wouldn’t say you—”

“We’ve talked enough, Benjamin.”

“Wait a minute. So you wouldn’t say you loved him.”

“Not exactly,” she said, slipping out of her skirt and putting it on the hanger.

“But you don’t hate him,” Benjamin said.

“No Benjamin, I don’t hate him. Undo my bra.” She backed up to the chair.

“You don’t hate him and you don’t love him,” Benjamin said, reaching up to unfasten the two straps of her bra.

“That’s right.”

“Well how do you feel about him then.”

“I don’t,” she said. She dropped the bra on the bureau.

"Well that's kind of a bad situation then, isn't it."

"Is it?"

"I mean it doesn't sound like it could be much worse. If you hated him at least you'd hate him."

She nodded and removed her slip.

"Well you loved him once, I assume," Benjamin said.

"What?"

"I say I assume you loved your husband once. When you first knew him."

"No," she said.

"What?"

"I never did, Benjamin. Now let's—"

"Well wait a minute," he said. "You married him."

She nodded.

"Why did you do that."

"See if you can guess," she said. She unfastened her stocking from their clasps* and began peeling them down* over her legs.

"Well I can't," Benjamin said.

"Try."

"Because of his money?"

"Try again," she said. She began forcing the girdle down around her legs.

"You were just lonely or something?"

"No."

Benjamin frowned. "For his looks?" he said. "He's a pretty handsome guy, I guess."

"Think real hard, Benjamin."

Benjamin frowned down at one of her feet, then shook his head. "I can't see why you did," he said, "unless ... you didn't *have* to marry him or anything, did you?"

"Don't tell Elaine," Mrs Robinson said.

"Oh no."

She nodded.

"You had to marry him because you got pregnant*?"

"Are you shocked?"

"Well," Benjamin said. "I never thought of you and Mr Robinson as the kind of people who ..." He shook his head.

"All right," she said. "Now let's go to bed."

"Wait a minute. Wait a minute. So how did it happen."

"What?"

clasps *here* fasteners which hold the stockings **to peel down** *here* to roll down over the legs **pregnant** expecting a child

"I mean do you feel like telling me what were the circumstances?"
"Not particularly."
"I mean what was the setup*. Was he a law student at the time?"
She nodded.
"And you were a student also."
"Yes."
"At college."
"Yes."
"What was your major."
She frowned at him. "Why are you asking me all this."
"Because I'm interested, Mrs Robinson. Now what was your major subject at college."
"Art."
"Art?"
She nodded.
"But I thought you—I guess you kind of lost interest in it over the years then."
"Kind of."
"So," Benjamin said. "You were an art major* and he was a law student. And you met him. How did you meet him. At a party or at a dance or—"
"I don't remember, Benjamin," she said, removing her bobby pins and shaking her head to let the hair fall down around her shoulders, "and I am getting pretty tired of this conversation."
"Well how did it happen. How did you get pregnant."
"How do you think."
"I mean did he take you up to his room with him? Did you go to a hotel?"
"Benjamin, what does it possibly matter."
"I'm curious."
"We'd go to his car," she said.
"Oh no."
"What?"
"In the car you did it?"
"I don't think we were the first."
"Well no," Benjamin said. "But it's—it's kind of hard to conceive* of you and Mr Robinson going at it in the car." He sat down in the chair again and began to smile. "In the car?" he said. "You and him?"
"Me and him."

setup background; circumstances **you were an art major** art was your main subject
to conceive of to think; to imagine

He shook his head, still smiling. "So that's where old Elaine—" He looked up. "What kind of car was it."

"What?"

"Do you remember the make of car*?"

"Oh my God."

"Really," Benjamin said "I want to know."

"It was a Ford, Benjamin."

"A Ford!" he said, jumping up from the chair. "A Ford!" He laughed aloud. "Goddammit, a Ford! That's great!"

"That's enough."

He shook his head and smiled down at the rug. "So old Elaine Robinson got started in a Ford."

"Benjamin?"

"That's great."

"Benjamin?"

"What."

"Don't talk about Elaine."

He stopped smiling suddenly. "Don't talk about Elaine?" he said.

"No."

"Why not?"

"Because I don't want you to," she said. She turned around and walked to the bed.

"Well why don't you."

Mrs Robinson pulled the bedspread down along the bed and dropped it on the floor.

"Is there some big secret about her I don't know?"

"No."

"Then what's the big mystery."

"Take off your clothes," she said.

Benjamin frowned and removed his coat. He dropped it behind him onto the chair, then began unbottoning his shirt.

"I wish you'd tell me," he said.

"There's nothing to tell."

"Well why is she a big taboo subject all of a sudden."

Mrs Robinson uncovered one of the pillows at the head of the bed.

"Well," Benjamin said, removing his shirt and dropping it on his coat, "I guess I'll have to ask her out on a date and find out what's—"

Mrs Robinson straightened up suddenly. She turned around to stare at him. "Benjamin don't you ever take that girl out," she said.

the make of car the type of car

"What?"
"Do you understand that."
"Well look, I have no intention of taking her out."
"Good."
"I was just kidding around*."
"Good."
"But why shouldn't I."
"Because you shouldn't."
"Well why are you getting so upset."
"Let's drop it," Mrs Robinson said. She turned back to the bed and uncovered the other pillow.
"Are you jealous of her?" Benjamin said. "Are you afraid she might steal me away from you?"
"No."
"Well then what."
She shook her head.
"Mrs Robinson," Benjamin said, taking a step toward her, "I want to know why you feel so strongly about this."
"I have my reasons."
"Then let's hear them."
"No."
"Let's hear your reasons, Mrs Robinson. Because I think I know what they are."
She reached down to pull the covers* part way back.
"Your daughter shouldn't associate with* the likes of me*, should she."
"Benjamin."
"I'm not good enough for her to associate with, am I. I'm not good enough to even talk about her, am I."
"Let's drop it."
"We're not dropping it, Mrs Robinson," he said, walking across the room. "Now that's the reason, isn't it. I'm a dirty degenerate, aren't I. I'm not fit to—"
"Benjamin?"
He took her arm and pulled her around to face him. "I'm good enough for you but I'm too slimy* to associate with your daughter. That's it, isn't it."
She nodded.
"Isn't it!"

to kid around to fool around **covers** sheet and blanket covering the bed **to associate with** to keep company with; to be together with **the likes of me** people like me **slimy** unpleasant; disgusting

"Yes."

He stood a moment longer holding her arm, then pushed her down on the bed. "You go to hell," he said. He shook his head and walked back to the chair to pick up his shirt. "You go straight to hell, Mrs Robinson."

"Benjamin?"

"Do you think I'm proud of myself?" he said, throwing the shirt down on the rug and walking back to stand in front of her. "Do you think I'm proud of this?"

"I wouldn't know."

"Well, I am not."

"You're not."

"No sir," he said. "I am not proud that I spend my time in hotel rooms with a broken-down alcoholic!"

"I see."

"And if you think I come here for any reason besides pure boredom, then you're all wrong."

She nodded.

"Because—Mrs Robinson?"

"What."

"You make me sick! I make myself sick! This is the sickest, most perverted thing that ever happened to me!" He stared down at her a moment. "And you do what you want but I'm getting the hell out."

"Are you?"

"You're goddamn right I am," he said. He turned around, picked up his shirt from the floor and slid his arms into its sleeves. Mrs Robinson sat up on the edge of the bed and watched him as he buttoned it and tucked* the shirttails* into his pants.

"Benjamin?" she said.

He shook his head.

"Did you mean those things you said, Benjamin?"

"You are damn right I did."

"I'm sorry," she said.

"Well, I am too. But that's the way it is."

"That's how you feel about me."

He nodded.

"That I'm a sick and disgusting person," she said, looking down at the rug. Benjamin finished tucking in his shirttails, then looked at her. "Now don't start this," he said.

"What?"

to tuck into *G* hineinstecken **shirt tails** loose ends of a shirt

"Don't start acting hurt*."

"Don't you expect me to be a little hurt?"

"Now Mrs Robinson," he said, pointing at her. "You told me yourself that you were an alcoholic."

She nodded. "And sick and disgusting," she said.

"Now wait a minute," he said. "You stand there and call me trash*. What do you expect me to say."

"Did I call you that?"

"You did."

"I don't think so," she said.

"Well in so many words, Mrs Robinson. You stand there and tell me I'm not good enough for your daughter."

"Did I say that?"

"Of course you did."

She shook her head.

"What?"

"Benjamin," she said, "I want to apologize to you if that's the impression you got."

"Well Mrs Robinson," he said. "Two minutes ago you told me I wasn't good enough for your daughter. Now you say you're sorry I got that impression."

"I didn't mean it," she said.

"What?"

"I don't think you'd be right for each other," she said. "But I would never say you weren't as good a person as she is."

"You wouldn't."

"Of course I wouldn't."

Mrs Robinson waited a moment, then stood and walked to the closet to remove her hanger of clothes.

"What are you doing."

"Well it's pretty obvious you don't want me around any more," she said.

"Well look," Benjamin said. "I was kind of upset there. I'm sorry I said those things."

"Benjamin, if that's how you feel—"

"But it's not."

"That's all right," she said, smiling at him. "I think I can understand why I'm disgusting to you."

"Oh no," Benjamin said. He hurried across the room. "Look," he said, taking her arm. "I like you. I wouldn't keep coming here if I didn't like you."

don't start acting hurt don't pretend to be hurt **trash** *here* worthless person

"But if it's sickening for you—"

"It's not!" he said. "I enjoy it. I look forward to it. It's the one thing I have to look forward to."

"You don't have to say that."

"Well I wouldn't. I would never say it if it wasn't true."

"May I stay then?" she said.

"Yes. Please. I want you to."

"Thank you."

"Well don't thank me, because I want you to."

She lifted the hanger back into the closet. "But you won't ever take out Elaine, will you."

"What?"

"I want you to promise me that."

Benjamin shook his head. "Look," he said. "Let's not talk about that. Let's not talk at all."

"Promise me."

"But why should I! Because I'm not good enough for her?"

"Because you're different."

"How are we different."

"You just are."

"She's good and I'm bad. Look. Why the hell did you bring this up. It never occurred* to me to take her out."

"Then give me your word you won't."

"But I don't like to give my word about things."

"Why not."

"Because you never know what's going to happen."

"Then you're thinking of taking her out, aren't you."

"No," Benjamin said. "I give you my word I have no intention of taking her out."

"Now give me your word that you never will."

"This is absurd."

"Promise me, Benjamin."

"All right, for Christ's sake! I promise I will never take out Elaine Robinson."

"You swear to it."

"Yes."

"Thank you."

"Now let's get the hell into bed."

to occur to s.o. to come into s.o.'s mind

5

It was several days later that the subject of Elaine Robinson was brought up again. It was at the Braddocks' dinner table.
"Elaine's back from school today," Mr Braddock said. "She just got back for the holidays."
Benjamin sprinkled some salt onto a piece of meat on his plate.
"Ben?" his father said.
"What."
"I think it might be a nice idea if you asked her out."
Benjamin stopped salting his meat. "What?"
"I think it might be a nice gesture if you asked her out to dinner sometime next week."
"Why should I do that," Benjamin said.
"Because I'd like you to."
"You would."
"Yes."
"Why would you like me to."
"Well Ben," his father said, "because they've shown an interest in you and done things for us and this is a good way to keep the relations between the two families smooth."
"You don't think they're smooth?"
"I think they could be smoother."
"They seem plenty smooth to me."
"Ben?" his mother said. "Don't you think she's a terribly attractive girl?"
"Yes I do," Benjamin said. "But that's not the point."
"Because I think she's one of the prettiest—"
"Mother, she is a beautiful girl," Benjamin said, putting the salt shaker back on the table. "But Elaine and I do not get along."
"How do you know."
"Because," Benjamin said, "I took her out once before."
"When."
"In high school."
"Five years ago?"
"Yes five years ago, Mother."
"And you did enjoy each other."
"No we did not."
"Well I'll bet it would be a lot different now," Mrs Braddock said.
"It would not," Benjamin said. "It was awkward and strained* five years ago and it would be awkward and strained now."

strained not natural, easy or relaxed

"Ben?" Mr Braddock said, wiping at the corner of his mouth with a napkin*. "It's awkward and strained for me every time Mr Robinson comes over here and you tell him you're going to call up his daughter."

"Well he asks me, for God's sake. What am I supposed to say: 'Hell no, I'm not'?"

"Look, Ben."

"He doesn't expect me to call her up, Dad. It's just small talk."

"You're wrong," Mr Braddock said, returning the napkin to his lap and looking up at his son. "He made a special point of telling me she was back. He made a special point of telling me to let you know."

"All right," Benjamin said. He picked up his knife and fork from beside his plate and began cutting the salted meat. "Next time he asks me I'll tell him I have no intention of ever calling her up in my life."

"You call her up after dinner."

Benjamin looked up and dropped the knife and fork on his plate. "What the hell is this," he said.

"Is your time so valuable, Ben?"

"That has nothing to do with it."

"Is your television viewing and evening drinking so important that you can't take one night out to do something for someone else?"

"Elaine Robinson and I do not get along!" he said. "Elaine Robinson and I have nothing in common!"

Mr Braddock nodded. "I guess she's not quite your intellectual equal, is she."

"Come on now."

"I guess it would be quite a strain to spend an entire evening with someone of inferior mentality*, wouldn't it."

"You know goddamn well that has nothing to do with it."

"Shhhh!" Mrs Braddock said. "Don't go on like this. Now if Benjamin absolutely refuses to take her out—"

"I do."

"All right then," Mrs Braddock said. "I'll invite the family over here to dinner."

"What?"

"I'll have the Robinsons over here to dinner some evening next week."

Benjamin frowned down at his plate.

"Any special objection to that?" his father said.

"No," Benjamin said. "Of course not."

napkin a small piece of cloth or paper for wiping one's lips at meals **of inferior mentality** less intelligent

He ate the rest of his dinner quietly. He waited while his mother cleared the table, then ate dessert and drank a cup of coffee.
"Excuse me," he said when he was finished. "I'll go call Elaine now."

Just after seven o'clock the following evening Benjamin removed a bottle of bourbon from the liquor cabinet, drank several large swallows, then wiped his mouth with the back of his hand. Several minutes later he parked his car at the curb in front of the Robinson's house and walked up the flagstone path to the front door. The night had already become dark and the porch light was turned on for him.
Mr Robinson opened the door almost the moment Benjamin rang.
"Well Braddock," he said, shaking his hand and grinning. "It's about time you got around to this."
Benjamin followed him into the house.
"I'm afraid the young lady isn't quite dressed yet," Mr Robinson said. He led Benjamin down the hall to the back of the house and into the sun porch. His wife was sitting in one of the chairs on the porch with a drink in her hand. She looked up at Benjamin when he appeared but didn't smile or attempt to rise from her chair.
"Hello," Benjamin said.
Mr Robinson had pushed his hands down into the pockets of his pants but now removed one of them almost immediately to glance at his watch.
"What would you say to a short one*," he said.
"All right."
"Bourbon still your drink?"
"Yes."
Benjamin waited until he had left the room, then turned back to Mrs Robinson, who was still sitting in the chair looking at the large glass panels enclosing the porch.
"Now listen," he said. "This was not my idea. It was my father's idea."
"Benjamin?" she said quietly, not looking at him. "Didn't I make myself perfectly clear about this?"
"I'm saying it was not my idea," he said, taking a step toward her. "I'm saying my parents thought it would be a nice little social gesture if I—"
"I thought I made myself quite clear to you."
"You did, Mrs Robinson."
"Then why are you here."
"Because it was either this or a dinner party for the two families. And I'm afraid I couldn't quite handle* that, if you don't mind."

a short one a quick drink of whisky **to handle** to manage

Mrs Robinson raised her glass to her lips.

"Now I'm taking her out this once," Benjamin said. "We'll go out to dinner and have a drink and I'll bring her back. That's it. I have no intention of ever taking your precious daughter out again in her life. So don't get upset about it."

"But I am," she said.

"What?"

"I'm extremely upset about it, Benjamin."

Mr Robinson came down the three steps leading onto the sun porch, carrying a drink for Benjamin and one for himself, which he took to a chair beside Mrs Robinson.

"Sit down," he said, gesturing at a chair. "Sit down."

Benjamin sat.

"Well," Mr Robinson said, raising his glass. "Here's to you and your date."

As he was drinking Benjamin looked over the rim* of his glass at Mrs Robinson. She was still sitting very straight in her chair looking out through the glass panels and into the dark back yard.

"Ben?" Mr Robinson said.

"What."

"How long has it been since you and Elaine have seen each other."

"I don't remember."

Elaine appeared at the entrance of the porch wearing a neat brown dress. She was carrying a green coat over one of her arms and reaching up trying to adjust a small gold earring.

"Hello," she said, smiling.

"Hello," Benjamin said. He glanced at her, then back down at the floor.

"What's the trouble there," Mr Robinson said.

"The clasp is broken on this," she said. She tried again to fix the earring into her ear, then frowned. "Do you mind if I don't wear these?" she said to Benjamin.

"No," he said.

Elaine removed the other earring and set them down in a glass ash tray. Then she seated herself. She folded the green coat in her lap.

"I was just asking Ben how long it's been since you two have seen each other," Mr Robinson said.

"I don't know," Elaine said. "Didn't we go out once in high school?"

"We did," Benjamin said.

Mr Robinson nodded and looked down at his drink, which he was holding in front of him in both hands. "Well," he said, grinning, "I want you to keep

rim edge

your wits about* you tonight. You never know what tricks Ben picked up back there in the East." He twirled his drink around in the glass, tasted it, then leaned back in his chair and looked at Benjamin. "Where did you think of going," he said.

"Sir?"

"Where did you think of going."

"Hollywood," Benjamin said.

"You're going to do the old town."

"What?"

"I say you're going to do the old town. Hit the big night spots*."

Benjamin finished his drink and set the empty glass on a table beside him. "Let's go," he said. He stood. Elaine stood and handed him her coat. As he was helping her on with it he happened to glance at the panel that was reflecting Mrs Robinson. Her eyes stared back evenly at him out of the glass. "We'll be back early," he said.

"Oh hell," Mr Robinson said. "You stay out as late as you want."

Benjamin slammed the door of his car after Elaine had gotten in, then walked around to seat himself under the steering wheel. He started the engine and turned away from the curb.

"My mother's in a strange mood today," Elaine said.

"What did she say."

"What?"

"I mean what are you talking about."

"My mother," Elaine said. "She's been in kind of a trance today for some reason. I think she must have something on her mind."

"What."

"I don't know what."

Benjamin turned his car onto a ramp* and drove down the ramp and out onto the freeway.

"You don't know her very well, do you," Elaine said.

"No."

"Because I'm afraid you must think she's awfully rude."

"Are you apologizing for her?"

"No," Elaine said. "I'm just—I'm afraid you might have gotten the wrong impression of her. But it's just this strange mood she's in today."

Benjamin pushed the accelerator of his car down to the floor and moved into the second lane. A car honked* behind him. Benjamin glanced into his mirror, then swerved* into the fast lane of traffic.

to keep one's wits about one to remain mentally alert **Hit the big night spots** go and see all the biggest night clubs **ramp** road joining a higher and a lower road **to honk** *G* (ungeduldig) hupen **to swerve** to turn to one side suddenly

"You're living at home now," Elaine said. "Is that right?"

"That's right."

She nodded. "Do you have any prospects* in mind?" she said.

"No."

"You don't have any jobs lined up*. Or graduate schools or anything."

Benjamin veered* back into the center lane, pressed on his horn and shot in front of the car he had been following. Elaine frowned at him a moment, then looked out through the windshield again.

"What about the prize you won," she said.

"What about it."

"What ever happened to that."

"I threw it away," Benjamin said.

"What?"

"I threw it away."

"Oh," Elaine said. "Why did you do that."

Benjamin sped up behind the bumper of the car traveling in front of him and began honking his horn. The man driving it held up his hand and began waving beside his head for Benjamin to stop honking. Benjamin stayed several inches behind him and continued to honk. Finally a space opened up in the next lane and the man swung into it. Benjamin shot ahead.

"Is anything wrong?" Elaine said.

"No."

"Do you always drive this way?"

"Yes."

Elaine looked back out through the front windshield.

The first night club they went to was called the Club Renaissance. Elaine handed her coat across a counter to a girl just inside the entrance. A man in a tuxedo showed them to a table in the center of the room. Except for someone seated by himself in the corner they were the only ones in the club. There was a bandstand* at the end of the room with a piano and a set of drums on it but no music was being played.

"Do you want some dinner?" Benjamin said when two drinks had been set on their table.

"I'd love some."

"Bring a menu," Benjamin said to the waiter.

"Dinner for two, sir?"

"No," Benjamin said. "Just for her."

The waiter nodded and disappeared.

prospect plan for the future **lined up** *here* arranged for you **to veer** to shift, turn
bandstand place for the band

"Aren't you eating?" Elaine said.

"No." Benjamin lifted his glass off the table and drank.

"Why not."

"If it's all right with you I'm not hungry."

The waiter returned a moment later with the menu but Elaine shook her head. "I've changed my mind," she said. "Thank you."

The name of the next night club was The Interior and there was a band playing as Elaine and Benjamin walked in through the front door. They found a table and Benjamin ordered two more drinks.

"Do you want to dance?" he said.

"Do you?"

Benjamin shrugged his shoulders and stood. Elaine stood and followed him onto the floor. They danced for several moments, then Benjamin dropped his hands to his sides and nodded at the table.

"The drinks have come," he said. He pushed his way back to the table through several couples.

In the next club there was a strip show. Elaine followed Benjamin through the door, removed her coat and checked* it. Benjamin walked across the room and selected a table immediately beneath the stage. He sat. When Elaine came to the table he nodded at the chair across from his.

"Benjamin?"

"Sit down."

"Well Benjamin?"

"What."

"Am I supposed to sit with the back of my head up against the stage?"

"You are."

"But couldn't we get a table farther back?"

"No."

Elaine waited a moment longer, then slid in onto the chair. When Benjamin had ordered drinks he pushed his hands into his pockets and slouched down* to watch the show.

A small band was playing on one side of the stage and in the center the stripper was bent over with her back to the audience, grinning at them between her legs. For a long time she stood flexing the muscles* in her buttocks* in time to the music, then she straightened up and began prancing* back and forth across the stage. Attached to the shiny cups over her nipples* were two long pink cords. At the end of each cord was a large pink tassel*. She began swinging them around in front of her as she walked.

to check *G* abgeben **to slouch down** to sit down in an unattractive way **to flex the muscles** *G* die Muskeln spielen lassen **buttocks** *G* Gesäß **to prance** to dance or jump about **nipples** *G* Brustwarzen **tassle** *G* Quaste

The waiter brought two drinks to Benjamin's table.

"Will you drink mine?" Elaine said.

"What for."

"I just wish you would."

"Are you drunk already?"

"Yes."

Benjamin picked her drink off the table, drained* it and returned it in front of her.

"Why don't you watch the show," he said.

She was sitting very straight in her chair, looking across the table at him.

"Benjamin?" she said.

"What."

"Do you dislike me?"

"What?"

"Do you dislike me for some reason?"

"No," Benjamin said. "Why should I."

"I don't know."

Benjamin settled back in his chair with the drink. The woman on the stage was still prancing around but instead of swinging the tassels she was holding them out in front of her. Suddenly she stopped and faced the audience. She dropped the tassels. The band stopped playing except for the drummer, who began rolling his drumsticks against the top of his drum. The stripper began swaying* one way, then the other, and the tassels began swaying back and forth with her. She swayed faster and faster until finally the tassels started swinging in circles around her breasts. Several of the customers began to applaud. Benjamin held his hands out in front of him and clapped.

"You're missing a great effect here," he said.

Elaine turned in her chair to watch the two tassels swinging around the woman's breasts, then turned back. She folded her hands in her lap and looked up into the smoky air over Benjamin's head.

"How do you like that," Benjamin said.

She didn't answer him.

"Could you do it?"

"No."

Suddenly the dancer caught one of the tassels and threw it around the other way so that the tassels were twirling around in opposite directions. The customers applauded. The woman slowly raised her arms out beside her and bent slightly forward. Then she walked to the front of the stage. Elaine was the

to drain to drink everything contained in a glass **to sway** to swing (from one side to another) only customer who had not brought her chair around to the side of the table facing the stage. The dancer walked over to where she was sitting and bent forward so the pink tassels began swinging down in front of Elaine's face. She winked at Benjamin, still holding her arms out beside her. Several men in the back began to laugh. Benjamin sat up in his chair and set the drink on the table. He frowned at the face of the dancer, then at Elaine, who was still sitting very straight in her chair looking up over Benjamin's head with the pink tassels crossing every few seconds in front of her face. She was crying. Benjamin stood suddenly and held one of his hands in the path of the tassels. They stopped swinging. A man in back began to boo. Benjamin took Elaine's hand and led her across the room to get her coat.

"Elaine?" he said when they were out on the sidewalk.

"Will you take me home now, please?"

"Elaine, I'm sorry."

She wiped one of her cheeks with the back of her hand. "I think I'd better go home now, please."

"But Elaine?"

"Which way is the car," she said. She put her hands in the pockets of her coat and looked down the sidewalk.

"Elaine, listen to me." She began walking ahead of him down the sidewalk.

"Elaine?"

"Please take me home," she said, walking faster and beginning to cry again.

"Well wait a minute," Benjamin said, catching up to her. "I'm sorry I took you in there."

"I want to go home!" She hurried ahead of him.

"Elaine," Benjamin said. He took her arm to stop her. "Now I want to tell you something."

"Take me home!"

"But could I just tell you one thing?"

"What."

"This whole idea," he said, still holding her arm. "This whole idea of the date and everything. It was my parents' idea. They forced me into it."

"Oh," Elaine said, reaching up to wipe her cheek again. "That's nice of you to tell me."

"But that's why I've been acting this way. I'm not like this. I hate myself like this."

"Can we go home now, please?"

"Well can't we have dinner or something?"

"No."

"Can we just sit somewhere and talk?"

"I want to go home!" she said, staring up into his face.

"But I want to just talk to you first."
"Benjamin, people are looking at us."
Benjamin glanced around, then led her away from the middle of the sidewalk and against a building. "Could you stop crying please?" he said.
"No I couldn't."
"But could you try?" — "No."
He looked down at her a moment, then put his other arm around her and brought her up close against him and kissed her. They stood without moving for several moments and then finally Elaine turned her face away and cleared her throat.
"People are still staring at us," she said quietly.
He tried to kiss her again but she turned her head.
"I don't want to do this in the public view," she said.
"We'll go to the car."
"Can we get something to eat?" she said.
He took her hand and led her down the sidewalk and into a restaurant. They were shown a table in the rear. As soon as they were seated Benjamin reached across the table and took her hand again.
"Elaine," he said.
"What."
"Are you all right now."
"Yes."
"And can you try and understand that I'm not like that. Like I was earlier."
She nodded.
"You can understand that."
"Here's the waitress."
A waitress had appeared beside their table with her pad of paper* and pencil.
"What do you want," Benjamin said.
"A hamburger."
"Right," Benjamin said to the waitress. "Two." The waitress wrote down the order and walked away from the table. Benjamin looked back at Elaine. For a long time he sat looking at her, then he began shaking his head.
"Elaine?" he said. "I just—I just wish you could see that I'm not like that. That's not the way I am at all."
"Well, are you sick or what," she said.
"Sick?"
"I mean why are you in such a poor mood."
"I don't know," he said. "It's this whole frame of mind I've been in ever since I graduated."

a pad of paper *G* Schreibblock

Elaine put her napkin down into her lap. They sat quietly until the waitress brought their food and set it in front of them. Benjamin picked up his hamburger, but immediately put it down. "I've had this feeling," he said. "Ever since I've been out of school I've had this overwhelming urge* to be rude all the time."

Elaine picked up her hamburger. "Why don't you go back to school then," she said.

"I'd flunk out*," Benjamin said.

Elaine began to eat her hamburger. Benjamin picked his up and raised it to his mouth, but then set it down on the plate again. "And I just feel badly," he said. "And I want to apologize to you. Because I'm not that way."

She nodded.

Benjamin looked down at the hamburger on his plate, then picked it up and raised it to his mouth.

It was not till after midnight that they finally drove up in front of the Robinsons' house and parked. For several moments they sat quietly beside each other in the car. Then Elaine turned her head toward him and smiled. "Would you like to come in?" she said. "I'll fix you a drink. Or some coffee."

Benjamin shook his head. "Actually," he said, "I'm not too thirsty."

Elaine nodded and again it was quiet. "Well," she said finally, "maybe I'd better go in now."

Benjamin took her hand. Then she turned to look at him and he brought her head forward and kissed her.

"Benjamin?" she said quietly when he was through.

"What, Elaine."

"Wouldn't the house be more comfortable?"

"Well I don't—I mean I wouldn't want to wake anyone up."

"We won't," she said, reaching for the handle of the door. "Let's go inside."

"Wait a minute," Benjamin said. He took her hand and pulled it back. "I mean why do you want to go inside."

"Because I think it would be more comfortable."

"Well, isn't the car comfortable?"

Elaine frowned at him. "Is anything wrong?" she said.

"What?"

"Why don't you want to go in the house."

"Oh," Benjamin said. "Well I was—I was thinking maybe we could do something else. Go somewhere."

"All right."

urge strong desire **to flunk out** to be sent away from a school or college because of failure

Benjamin started the engine of his car.

"Where are we going," Elaine said.

"A bar. I'm trying to think of a bar around here."

"Isn't there one in the Taft Hotel?" Elaine said.

Benjamin looked at her.

"Isn't there?" she said.

"I can't—I can't remember."

"Let's go there," she said.

"The Taft?"

She nodded.

"Well wait a minute," he said, beginning to shake his head. "I mean isn't that pretty far?"

"It's only a mile," she said.

"A mile," Benjamin said. "But there might not be a bar."

"Let's go see."

"But Elaine," he said. "I mean why did—why did you say the Taft."

She turned in her seat to look at him again. "What is the matter," she said.

"Well nothing," he said. "I'm just—I'm just wondering if they have a bar or not. I mean let's go see. Let's go see if they do or not."

They walked in through the door of the Verandah Room and Elaine chose the table in the corner by the window. Benjamin helped her off with her coat and they sat. Elaine looked out the window at the grounds for a few moments, then turned back to Benjamin. "I have the feeling I've been here before," she said. "Don't they have a ballroom here?"

"I don't know."

"I think they do," she said. "I think I came to a party here once."

Benjamin nodded without looking at her. Elaine opened her mouth to say something more, then suddenly began frowning towards the entrance of the bar. She leaned forward and rested her hand on one of Benjamin's sleeves.

"There's a man over there that keeps staring at us," she said.

Benjamin shook his head.

"One of the elevator operators," she said. "He stared at us when we came in and he still is."

"Elaine, let's go."

"Look," she said. "There's two of them. They're talking about us."

"Elaine—"

"They're just standing in the doorway staring at us and talking together. One of them pointed at us."

Suddenly a waitress placed two drinks in front of them, then disappeared.

Elaine looked up and frowned after her. "What's happening," she said.

Benjamin cleared his throat.

"Benjamin?"

"Elaine, let's go now."

"Why did she bring us these drinks."

"I ordered as we came in the door."

"No you didn't."

"Just drink it, please."

"What?"

"Just drink your drink, please."

"But she made a mistake."

Benjamin shook his head. "She didn't," he said. "I ordered as we came in the door."

"You did not."

"Elaine, I did," he said. "I said it to her quietly as we passed her."

"Why are you saying that."

"Because I did!" Benjamin said.

"You didn't."

"Will you please drink it!"

She looked down at the drink on the table in front of her. "This isn't what I wanted," she said.

"Goddammit!" Benjamin said. He reached across the table for the drink, which was a martini, and drank it quickly.

"Benjamin, what is happening."

"Nothing."

"Well something is," she said. "What is it."

"I just don't like this place," Benjamin said.

"Why not."

"Because I don't."

"Well why did you lie to me about ordering the drinks."

"I didn't."

"Then why are you so upset."

"Let's get out!" Benjamin said. He stood suddenly, jarring the table with his knees, and took Elaine's coat off the empty chair at the side of the table. He dug into his pocket for some money to drop on the table, then reached for Elaine's hand. "Come on, come on."

He hurried ahead of her out of the Verandah Room and into the lobby. One of the clerks stopped when he saw him and smiled. "Good evening, Mr Gladstone," he said. Benjamin rushed past him.

"Benjamin?" Elaine said.

"Come on!" He pulled her toward the entrance of the hotel.

"Benjamin? Do they know you here or something?"

They walked out across the pavilion in front of the hotel and to the parking

lot. Benjamin opened the door of his car for her and pushed the coat into her hands. "Please get in," he said.
"But Benjamin?"
"Goddammit, will you get in this car!"
She got into the car. Benjamin closed the door after her and walked around to the other side. As soon as he was inside and the door was closed he put his hands up over his face. For a long time he sat shaking his head with his hands covering his eyes. "Elaine?" he said finally. "I like you. I like you so much."
She watched him but didn't answer.
"Do you believe that, Elaine?"
She nodded.
"Do you?"
"Yes."
"You're the first—you're the first thing for so long that I've actually liked. The first person I could actually stand to be with."
She reached up and took one of his hands down from his face.
"I mean my whole life is such a waste. It's just nothing, Elaine." He waited a moment longer, then pulled his hand away from her and shook his head. "I'm sorry," he said, reaching into his pocket for the keys of his car. "I'll take you home."
She watched him fit the key into the ignition switch* and turn on the engine.
"Benjamin?" she said.
"What, Elaine."
"Are you having an affair with someone?"
Benjamin stared at his hand on the key.
Elaine shook her head. "I'm sorry," she said.
"Elaine?"
"I'm sorry," she said again. "It's not my business."
Benjamin slowly turned the key and the engine stopped. He sat staring at his hand for several moments, then looked up slowly and out of the windshield of his car. "It just happened," he said. "It was just this shabby thing that happened along with everything else." He looked at her. "Can you understand that? Can you understand that, Elaine?"
She nodded.
"But what do you think of me now."
"What?"
"Do you think anything of me now?"
She nodded.
"But what do you think."

ignition switch *G* Zündschloß

Elaine shrugged. "I think you had an affair with someone," she said. "What else am I supposed to think."

"But don't you despise me?"

She frowned at him.

"Don't you?"

She took his hand again. "Benjamin?" she said, her eyes on his hand. "Was she married or something?"

He nodded.

"With a family?"

"A son. She had a husband and a son."

"Well, did they ever find out?"

"No."

"And it's all over now?"

"Yes."

Elaine shook her head. "Why should I despise you," she said.

"But Elaine," he said, turning to look at her. "I mean what if—what if it was someone you knew. How would you feel then."

"I don't know," she said.

"Would you hate me then?"

"I don't think so," she said. "Was it?"

"What?"

"Is it someone I know?"

"No."

"Just a woman you met in a bar?"

Benjamin nodded.

"Well, was she bored and lonely and everything?"

"She was."

"Then I suppose you relieved the boredom," Elaine said. "I mean I don't think it's my business. I'm sorry I found out."

"You are?"

"Well it seems to upset you that I did."

"Elaine, it doesn't upset me," he said. "But would you—would you go out with me again if I asked you? After knowing about it?"

"I think so."

"Well then, can I ask you out?"

"If you want."

"Tomorrow? Can we do something tomorrow?"

"All right," she said.

"During the day," Benjamin said. "We'll go for a drive or something during the day then."

She nodded.

"And you're sure you really want to. I wouldn't want you to do it unless you really wanted to."

"I do," she said.

"You do."

"Benjamin, I really do," she said.

In the morning the sky was a bright blue and there was not a single cloud. On the Robinsons' street the only sound was of a power lawnmower* being pushed back and forth across the Robinsons' front yard by a gardener. Benjamin parked his car, got out and walked quickly across the lawn to the door. He knocked and waited. Several moments later the door was opened by Mrs Robinson. She was wearing a green housecoat. Benjamin stood looking at her, glanced over her shoulder into the house, then looked back at her face.

"Elaine and I are going for a drive today," he said.

Mrs Robinson stepped out onto the front porch and pulled the door shut behind her. "Shall we talk in your car?" she said. "I'd rather not talk in the house."

"Well I'm not really sure there's anything to—"

"Elaine is still asleep." Mrs Robinson slid her hands into the pockets of her housecoat. She stepped down from the porch and began walking across the lawn toward Benjamin's car, nodding at the gardener as she passed him. She reached the car and got in. Benjamin stood watching her as she closed the door after her and folded her arms across her chest. Finally he shook his head and walked past the gardener to the side of his car.

"Mrs Robinson?"

"Get in, Benjamin," she said without looking at him.

"I really don't think there's much to say, Mrs Robinson."

"Get in this car."

Benjamin waited a few moments longer, then walked around to get in under the steering wheel.

"Drive down the block," she said, pointing ahead of them through the window.

Benjamin started the engine. "Mrs Robinson," he said, "I hope you won't be offended if I say I think you're being a little melodramatic about this. I don't think there's any great crisis that calls for—"

"Drive several houses down and park."

Benjamin released* the emergency brake* and drove slowly along the curb until he was several houses away. Then he stopped the car and turned off the

power lawnmower electric machine for cutting the grass **to release** to let go of **emergency brake** handbrake; *G* Handbremse engine and sat back in his seat. For several moments it was perfectly quiet except for the noise of the lawnmower behind them.

"Benjamin, I'm sorry it's come to this," Mrs Robinson said finally.

Benjamin nodded.

"But I'm telling you never to see her again."

He nodded a second time.

"Do I make myself clear?"

"Yes you do."

"I'm glad," Mrs Robinson said. "Why don't we consider the matter closed then."

"Because it's not closed."

"Isn't it?"

"No it's not," Benjamin said, closing his hands around the bottom part of the steering wheel. "I have no intention of following your orders, Mrs Robinson."

"Benjamin?"

"Why don't you tell me exactly what your objections are, Mrs Robinson. Instead of—"

"Do you want me to?"

"Yes I do."

"Well Benjamin?" she said. "Elaine is a very simple girl. She is sweet and she is uncomplicated."

"Mrs Robinson?"

"But she is thoroughly honest, Benjamin. She is thoroughly sincere." She shook her head. "And Benjamin?" she said. "You are none of these things."

"Mrs Robinson?"

"What."

"What time does she usually get up."

"Well Benjamin, I don't think you need to worry about that."

"I think I do," Benjamin said. "I think we have a date and I think she's expecting me."

"I'll explain to her that you couldn't make it."

"No you won't."

"Benjamin?" she said, turning suddenly in her seat. "You are to go home now. You are to go home and never come back to this house."

"Go to hell."

"Don't be cute*, Benjamin."

"I'm not, Mrs Robinson."

"Because I'll make things most unpleasant if I have to."

cute funny

"You will."

"Yes I will."

Benjamin nodded. "Could I ask you what you plan to do, Mrs Robinson?"

"Do I have to tell you?"

"Yes you do."

"Well Benjamin?" she said, looking at the side of his face. "I'll tell Elaine everything I have to in order to keep her away from you."

It was quiet for several moments.

"I don't believe you," Benjamin said finally.

"Then you'd better start believing me."

"I don't think you could do that, Mrs Robinson. I don't think you could tell her that."

"I hope I don't have to."

Benjamin turned suddenly in his seat. "You can't do that," he said, taking her wrist. "You can't do that, Mrs Robinson."

She stared back at him.

"Mrs Robinson," he said, shaking his head, "I'm asking you not to do that. I'm asking you please not to do that."

"Go home now," she said. She pulled her wrist away.

"Mrs Robinson, don't wreck it*. I'm asking you please not to wreck it!"

Benjamin stared at her several moments, then turned suddenly toward the door. He grappled* for the handle and threw it open. Then he jumped quickly out into the street. A car swerved around him, honking its horn. Without closing the door of his car he hurried back up the street to the Robinsons' house and past the gardener, who stopped mowing the lawn to watch him. The front door was locked. He ran around the house and in through the kitchen.

"Elaine!"

He ran through the kitchen and the dining room.

"Elaine! Elaine!"

A door opened upstairs. Benjamin ran part way up the carpeted stairs.

"Elaine!"

"Benjamin?"

"I'm coming up, Elaine!"

"Well, could you wait till I'm dressed?" she said. "I'll be right down."

Benjamin hurried to the top of the stairs. Elaine was standing in a doorway at the end of the hall. He rushed the length of the hall to where she was and took her hand to pull her back into the room.

"What is the matter," she said.

don't wreck it *here* don't destroy it **to grapple** to seize desperately

"I want you to meet me on the corner," Benjamin said, trying to catch his breath. "I want you to go over the back fence and I'll pick you up on the next street."

"What are you talking about."

"Will you please do that!"

"No," she said, frowning at him.

"Please!"

"What is happening."

He began dragging her toward the door but she pulled away from him.

"I'm not even dressed, Benjamin."

"You are."

"My shoes."

"Well get them on."

"Do you mind if I eat breakfast before we go?"

"Get the shoes on," Benjamin said. "I'll be right back." He ran out the door and down the hall to one of the rooms in the front of the house. He hurried to a window overlooking the front yard and threw aside the curtain just in time to see Mrs Robinson appear. She was walking quickly up the street. She walked up onto the lawn. Benjamin turned and ran back through the hall. Elaine was standing in her doorway.

"Why aren't your shoes on!"

"Because I want to know what's happening, Benjamin."

Benjamin hurried past her and into the room. The shoes were beside the bed. He picked them up. "Will you come on!" he said.

"No," she said. She stood in the center of the room scowling at him.

"Elaine!" Benjamin said.

Suddenly a door slammed downstairs. Benjamin looked up, stood very still for a few seconds, then dropped the shoes on the floor and took one of Elaine's hands. "Elaine," he said, "I have to tell you something."

"What."

"That woman."

"What?"

"That woman, Elaine. The older woman."

"What are you talking about."

"Elaine," Benjamin said, shaking his head, "it wasn't just some woman."

"What?"

"It wasn't just some woman with a husband and a son."

"Who was it then?"

Mrs Robinson appeared in the doorway and stopped. Elaine looked at her and then back at Benjamin. "Will somebody please tell me what is—" Suddenly she stopped talking. Her head turned slowly back toward her mother. Mrs

Robinson looked down at the floor, then cleared her throat quietly and left the room. Elaine pulled her hand away from Benjamin but continued staring through the empty doorway.

"Elaine?"

"Oh my God."

"Elaine?"

"Oh my God," she said again. She looked for a moment at Benjamin, then walked slowly to her window. She stared out through the glass at a house on the other side of the driveway. For a long time it was perfectly quiet. Finally Benjamin took a step toward her. "Elaine?" he said.

She spun around* to face him. "Get out of here!" she said.

"But Elaine?"

She rushed across the room to him and began pushing him toward the door. "Get out!" she said.

"But Elaine?"

"Get out! Get out of this house!" She pushed him as far as the doorway and then out through it, slamming the door shut. Then it was perfectly silent again.

Benjamin stood with his head tilted* slightly to the side, staring at Mrs Robinson, who was at the end of the hallway still wearing her green housecoat and standing very straight and motionless, staring back at him.

"Elaine?" he said quietly.

"Oh my God!" Elaine said from the other side of the door.

"Benjamin?" Mrs Robinson said to him from the end of the hall. "Goodbye." She turned around and disappeared into a room and closed the door behind her.

For several weeks Benjamin stayed at home. Sometimes he would go out by the pool and look down into the water and sometimes he would walk slowly around the block. But usually he sat in his room staring down at the rug or looking out through the window at some wires he could see running along beside the street on telephone poles. Then after he had been home for nearly a month and Christmas had passed and the new year had started he decided to marry Elaine.

to spin around to turn quickly **tilted** bent

Part Three

6

On the morning after he had made his decision Benjamin got up early. He took a shower and then found a small suitcase in the attic* that he had used at college and filled it with clothes and two sheets. He carried the suitcase and the pillow from his bed downstairs, and into the kitchen to wait for his parents to get up. When his father came in Benjamin had finished a small breakfast and was sitting at the table with his hands folded in his lap.

"You're up early," Mr Braddock said. He noticed the suitcase on the floor with the pillow resting on top of it and was about to say something more when Benjamin interrupted him.

"I'm going to marry Elaine Robinson," he said.

"What?"

"I'm going to marry Elaine Robinson," he said again.

Mr Braddock stood a moment longer where he was, then walked very slowly to the table and eased himself down into the chair across from his son.

"Are you serious?" he said.

Benjamin nodded.

"You are serious."

"Yes."

Mr Braddock slowly extended his hand. Benjamin shook it.

"I'll go tell your mother," Mr Braddock said. "Wait here." He stood and hurried out of the kitchen. Benjamin cleared his throat and folded his hands again in his lap.

Mrs Braddock came into the kitchen wearing her bathrobe. "What is all the excitement about," she said.

"Tell your mother," Mr Braddock said.

"I'm going to marry Elaine Robinson."

"What?"

She frowned at Benjamin, then at Mr Braddock.

"Ben and Elaine," Mr Braddock said. "He says they're getting married."

Mrs Braddock stared back at Benjamin, then began shaking her head. "Oh Ben," she said. She held out her arms. Benjamin stood and walked to her. She hugged him. "Oh Ben," she said, "I'm crying."

attic space or room(s) below the roof

Mr Braddock pulled a white handkerchief out of his pocket. "Now let him go," he said, handing it to his wife. "Let's get the whole story here." Mrs Braddock took the handkerchief to dry her eyes. Benjamin returned to his chair.

"Now," Mr Braddock said. He turned a chair around and straddled it backwards*. "Have you set the date yet."

"No."

Mrs Braddock sat down and reached for one of her son's hands.

"Have you told the Robinsons yet," Mr Braddock said.

"No."

"Let's call them right now."

"No."

"You want to wait on that."

"Oh Ben," Mrs Braddock said. She began crying again.

Benjamin cleared his throat. "I think I should tell you," he said, "that Elaine doesn't know about this yet."

Mrs Braddock stopped dabbing* at her eyes and lowered the handkerchief slowly from her face.

"She doesn't know about what yet," Mr Braddock said.

"That we're getting married."

"What?"

"I just decided an hour ago to marry her."

Mr Braddock glanced at his wife, then back at Benjamin. "Well you've certainly talked it over with her."

Benjamin shook his head.

"But you've written her about it."

"No."

"Called her?"

"No."

"Well good God, Ben," Mr Braddock said. "You get us all excited here, now you're saying you haven't even proposed?"

"That's what I'm saying."

Mr Braddock stood. He looked down at the suitcase on the floor. "What's all this about," he said, pointing at it.

"I'm driving up to Berkeley today."

"To propose to her?"

"That's right."

"Well," Mr Braddock said, taking his handkerchief back from his wife and

to straddle a chair backwards to sit astride (i.e., on a chair with the legs on each side)
to dab one's eyes to wipe one's eyes gently in order to dry them

stuffing it into his pocket, "this sounds kind of half-baked. What are you taking your gear* up for."

"I'm moving up there."

"To live?"

"Yes."

"Ben?" Mrs Braddock said, frowning at him. "We thought you meant—"

"Wait a minute," Mr Braddock said. "She's up there finishing school. You plan to just go up there and live near her?"

"Yes."

Mr Braddock shood his head. "Ben, you can't do that."

"That's what I'm doing."

"You sit down and write her a letter," Mr Braddock said. "Call her on the phone. But you can't go up there and pester* that girl just because you have nothing better to do."

"I love her," Benjamin said. He stood and leaned down to kiss his mother's cheek. Then he picked up the suitcase and pillow from the floor.

"Ben, listen to me," his father said. "I'm sure you do love her. And I think this is a fine thing. You and Elaine. But good God, man!"

Benjamin walked to the door.

"But you hardly know the girl, Ben. How do you know she wants to marry you."

"She doesn't yet."

"Well does she—does she like you?"

"No."

"Well for God's sake, Ben," Mr Braddock said, taking a step toward him and holding up one of his hands. "You can't just barge up* there and into her life like this."

Benjamin opened the door. "I'll send my address," he said.

"Ben?"

It was late in the afternoon when he drove into Berkeley and the streets were jammed with cars and people dodging* in and out between them. He found his way to the main street of the town, parked in front of a hotel and got out. For a moment he stood watching students passing back and forth on the sidewalk in front of him then pushed open the door of the hotel and walked in. An old man behind a desk looked up over the top of his newspaper.

"Do you have any rooms left for tonight," Benjamin said.

The man nodded.

your gear *here* your things **to pester** to annoy **to barge (up) into** to enter rudely **to dodge** to move quickly

"And do they have a phone."

"Some do."

"Good," Benjamin said. "I'll get my bag out of the car." He turned around but then stopped and walked back to the desk.

"Are there any good restaurants around here," he said. "Quiet ones."

"Go down to the corner."

Benjamin walked out of the hotel and down the sidewalk to the corner. He read carefully a menu* taped* onto the glass outside the restaurant, then went in and looked around at the tables in the center of the room and the booths* at the side. A waitress approached him with a menu.

"I wonder if I should make a reservation if I want to eat dinner here later."

"You can if you'd like," she said.

"But does it get crowded here. Around eight o'clock."

"It's hard to tell," she said.

Benjamin nodded. "I'll make one then," he said.

"Your name?"

"Braddock. Mr Braddock."

"And how many in your party."

"Just two," Benjamin said.

"Two."

"Yes," Benjamin said. "And I wonder if we could have that table over there." He pointed to the booth in the farthest corner of the room.

"Of course."

In Benjamin's hotel room there was a telephone on a table beside the bed. After he had been shown into the room he sat down beside it and for a long time stared down at the telephone without picking up the receiver. Finally he picked it up but put it down quickly before there was an answer from the operator. He stood and walked to the window. On the sidewalk below students were walking back and forth and in and out of stores or standing in small groups talking. Benjamin put his hands in his pockets and watched them awhile, then removed his clothes and took a shower. After he had put on clean clothes and had carefully combed his hair, he sat down again on the bed beside the telephone. He cleared his throat and picked up the receiver.

"Hello," he said to the operator. "Could you please give me the number of Elaine Robinson. She's a senior at the university."

It was quiet for several moments.

"She lives in Wendell Hall," the operator said finally.

"I see," Benjamin said.

"Shall I connect you, sir?"

menu list of dishes in a restaurant **taped onto** fixed to, stuck on **booth** *G* Nische

Benjamin opened his mouth but then closed it without answering.

“Sir?”

He cleared his throat.

“Shall I connect you?”

No,” he said. “No thank you. I’ll call back later.”

He ate dinner by himself in the coffee shop beside the hotel. When he finished he sat drinking coffee until just eight o’clock. Then he paid for his meal and walked out onto the sidewalk.

“Excuse me,” he said to a student. “Could you tell me where Wendell Hall is, please.”

The student pointed down the street. “Go down there and turn,” he said. “It’s a big quadrangle.”

Benjamin found his way to the dormitory* but instead of going inside he read the name over the door and then sat down on a bench in the center of the quadrangle. He sat a long time looking down at the cement at his feet and glancing up quickly every time a girl came out the door. Finally he got up and walked out of the quadrangle and back to town. After he had sat for over an hour in a restaurant drinking beer and watching the other patrons, he got up and returned to the dormitory and went inside to a lobby. A girl looked up from behind a desk at him.

“Does Elaine Robinson live in here,” he said.

The girl looked down at a list in front of her and nodded. “Room two hundred,” she said. “Shall I call her down?”

“Yes,” Benjamin said.

She reached for a telephone on her desk but just as she was about to dial, Benjamin held up one of his hands and began shaking his head.

“I just—I just remembered something I have to do.”

“You don’t want me to call her down?”

“No,” Benjamin said, taking a step backward.

“Is there a message?”

“No. No thank you. I just remembered this thing I have to do.” He turned around and hurried out of the dormitory and back to town and inside a movie theater across the street from his hotel.

In the morning Benjamin found a rooming house* several blocks from Elaine’s dormitory and moved into a room on the second floor. Then he sold his car. A used car lot* in town paid him twenty-nine hundred dollars in cash for it. He carried the money back to his room, put it in a drawer of his desk, then lay

dormitory *AE* building where students live **rooming house** house with furnished rooms to let **used car lot** garage which buys and sells second-hand cars down on his bed and spent the rest of the afternoon on his back staring up at the ceiling.

After a week he had still not seen Elaine. He walked several times each day past her dormitory, glancing at the girls going in and out of the front door, and often he sat on a bus bench across from the quadrangle watching them but not once did he see her. One afternoon he decided to ask the girl in the lobby to call her down again but as soon as he got inside the quadrangle he changed his mind and decided instead to write her a letter. At a drugstore across the street from his room be bought two quarts of beer and took them up to his room. He opened one and removed his stationery from the desk drawer and began to write.

Dear Elaine,
I am now living in Berkeley, after growing somewhat weary of family life. I have been meaning to stop by and pay my respects but am not entirely certain just how you feel about seeing me, after the incident involving myself and your mother. It was certainly a serious mistake on my part but not serious enough, I hope, to alter permanently your feelings about me. Your friendship means a great deal to me and it would be a burden off my mind to know that

Benjamin read over what he had written, then leaned back in the chair with the quart of beer and drank it slowly, staring over the desk and out the window at the roof of a house across the street. When the first quart was gone he dropped it in the wastebasket and opened the second. When the second was gone he dropped it on the floor, went to the bathroom, then returned to his desk and began a new letter.

Dear Elaine,
I love you and I can't help myself and I am begging you to forgive me for what I did. I love you so much I am terrified of seeing you every time I step out the door I cringe in terror* that you will be there please help me please forget what I did I am helpless and hopeless and lost and miserable please help me please dear Elaine forget what I did please o god dear Elaine I love you I love you forget what I

Benjamin got up without finishing the letter and fell down on his bed and went to sleep.

The next day he saw her.

He had just finished eating lunch at the university cafeteria and when he stepped out the door he saw her walking across a large pavilion below him, carrying an armload of books. He stopped and stared at her until she had passed the cafeteria, then hurried down the steps and followed her. She was walking quickly. Benjamin stayed several students behind her and turned to

to cringe in terror to be extremely terrified

follow her up some steps and into a large building. She stopped at a drinking fountain. Benjamin stopped and watched her as she drank. When she finished drinking he followed her down a long hall. She turned in through the door of a classroom. Benjamin walked quickly past the open door and glanced in to see her setting her books down on the armrest of one of the seats and saying something to someone seated beside her. He stopped on the other side of the door.

"Excuse me," he said to a girl as she turned into the classroom.

"What?"

"How long is this class."

"What?"

"This class," Benjamin said. "How long does it last."

"An hour," she said.

Outside the building there were benches and several trees. Benjamin returned to the cafeteria to buy a newspaper, then for an hour moved from one bench to another, smoking cigarettes and glancing at the headlines of the newspaper. When the hour was over a bell rang inside the building. Benjamin stood. Students began appearing at the entrance of the building and walking in small groups down the steps. Benjamin moved next to a tree and looked quickly from the face of one student to the next as they came out. Elaine appeared carrying her books in her arms and talking to another girl. They stopped. Elaine said something to her and laughed, then left her at the top of the steps and began to descend. Benjamin tucked his paper under his arm. He pushed his hands down into his pockets and cleared his throat, then walked away from the tree and toward Elaine, looking straight ahead of him. Just as he reached her he stopped and turned. Elaine stopped suddenly and stood staring at him. Benjamin looked down at the pavement. For several seconds he cleared his throat.

"Well," he said finally. "Elaine."

She didn't say anything.

"Well," Benjamin said, beginning to nod but still not looking up at her. "How—how are you. Are you fine?"

A student passing by bumped* him from behind. Benjamin turned to smile and nod at him. Then he cleared his throat again and looked back down at a point on the pavement beside Elaine's shoes. "I thought—I thought I might be seeing you. I thought I remembered you were going to school up here." He glanced up at her for a moment. She was still standing with her arms wrapped around the books and staring at him. He looked quickly down again. "I guess … I guess … let's see what time it is." He turned around and looked up

to bump *here* to knock

at a large clock on a tower beyond several buildings. "Yes," he said. "Well I've got to go now. Goodbye."

He hurried away from her, bumping into a student, then into another, then dodging in between several more and finally breaking away from the crowd and moving quickly back past the cafeteria building and to the street. A car honked at him and he jumped back up on the curb. He walked two blocks without stopping, then turned around and walked back across the block he had just covered and stopped in the center of the sidewalk to stare a moment at the passing traffic. Then he felt someone knock against him and he walked to a large wall at the edge of the sidewalk and slowly raised his hands up to cover his face.

He saw her again several days later. It was a Saturday afternoon and it was raining. Benjamin was taking a walk. He had walked several blocks down from the university and along a broad street with stores on it and awnings* that he went under when he wanted to get out of the rain. Elaine was standing at a bus stop. She was wearing a thin transparent raincoat and a small hat of the same plastic material over her hair. When he saw her Benjamin stopped suddenly and removed his hands from his pockets and looked at her a long time without moving. Then he hurried into a restaurant next to where she was standing. He sat down at a table beside the window and ordered a bottle of beer from the waitress. When it came he drank it quickly. There were large letters painted on the glass of the window. Sometimes he bent his head slightly to look around a huge green M at Elaine still standing in the rain at the bus stop, but usually he sat perfectly straight in the chair so that the M was directly between his face and Elaine.

When he had finished the first bottle of beer he ordered another. While he was drinking it a bus pulled up to the curb and stopped. Benjamin stood quickly and looked out over the top of the M. The doors of the bus opened but Elaine shook her head at the driver and then the doors closed and the bus moved on. The waitress was standing beside his table.

"Will that be all?" she said.

"No," he said. "One more."

She nodded.

"Where's the men's room."

"In the rear, sir."

Benjamin hurried to the back of the restaurant and into the men's room. He went to the bathroom and combed his hair, then returned to his table and quickly drank the bottle of beer waiting for him. When it was finished he stood and walked out of the restaurant and back into the rain. Elaine was

awning *G* Markise

standing at the edge of the sidewalk looking at a storefront on the other side of the street. Benjamin cleared his throat and walked toward her. Several feet behind her he stopped, cleared his throat again, and smiled. "Elaine?" he said, leaning slightly forward.

She turned around quickly.

Benjamin nodded. "I was just … I was just on a walk," he said. "I thought it was you."

"Hey!"

He turned around. There was a man in his shirt sleeves standing just outside the doorway of the restaurant holding a menu over his head to keep off the rain. "Want to pay for your beer?" he said.

"Oh," Benjamin said. He hurried back across the sidewalk and reached into his pocket for some money. He handed several dollar bills to the man, who took them and crumpled them in his free hand. "Is that a college trick?" he said.

"What?"

"Drink up and walk out? Is that a college trick?"

"No. I'm sorry." He turned around and walked back to Elaine.

"What are you doing here," she said.

"What?"

"What are you doing in Berkeley."

"Oh," Benjamin said. "Well I'm living here. Temporarily."

Elaine frowned at him a moment longer, then looked down the street.

"Waiting for a bus?" Benjamin said.

She nodded without looking at him.

"Well," Benjamin said. "Where—where might you be going."

"The city," she said.

Benjamin leaned forward and looked down the street. Several blocks away through the rain was the bus. "I might—I might ride in with you," he said. "If you—if you wouldn't mind too much."

"Hey!"

The man from the restaurant was standing outside again holding the menu over his head. "Your change," he said.

Benjamin smiled at him and nodded. "Keep it," he called.

"What?" — "You can have it."

The man stood frowning at him and holding out the change in one of his hands. Finally Benjamin hurried back across the sidewalk and the man dropped the money into his hand.

"Thank you," Benjamin said. He put the change in his pocket and returned to the other side of the sidewalk to wait quietly beside Elaine until the bus moved in beside the curb and opened its doors.

It was crowded, so they could not sit together. Elaine chose a seat near the center next to an old woman holding a closed umbrella in her lap and Benjamin walked past her and wedged* himself in between two old men on the broad seat in the rear of the bus.

On the other side of the long bridge spanning the bay the bus moved quickly down a causeway* and into a terminal*. Benjamin stood and followed Elaine out the front door and onto a platform.

"Well," he said, walking beside her along a ramp leading into the main part of the terminal. "Where might you be headed from here*."

"What?"

"I say where are you headed from here."

"I'm meeting someone," she said.

"A date*?"

"Yes."

Benjamin stopped to avoid colliding with a man coming the other way, then dodged around him and caught up with Elaine again.

"Right here?" he said, pointing down in front of him.

"What?"

"You're meeting him right here in the terminal?"

"No."

"Where," he said, hurrying to keep up with her.

"What?"

"I say where are you meeting him."

"At the zoo," she said.

"The zoo," Benjamin said. He cleared his throat. "They have a pretty good one here, do they?"

"I've never been to it."

"Oh," Benjamin said. "Well, I haven't either. I might … I might just ride out there with you. Keep you company on the ride."

They waited quietly on another platform for the bus to the zoo. Benjamin stood with his hands in his pockets, squinting up at the rain and sometimes leaning forward and craning* his head around the others on the platform to look for the bus. When it came he followed Elaine on and walked back with her to a free seat. She sat and removed the plastic hat to hold in her lap. Benjamin sat beside her.

"It's not—it's not much of a day for the zoo," he said, smiling.

(he) wedged himself in between … *G* (er) klemmte sich zwischen … **causeway** road surrounded by water **terminal** bus station **Where might you be headed from here** where are you going … **date** *AE G* Verabredung; Person, mit der man verabredet ist **to crane** to stretch out

"No, it's not," she said. She turned her head to look out through the wet glass of the window.

They rode without talking for several stops. Benjamin sat looking down at the seat in front of him and Elaine sat with her head turned toward the window looking out at the buildings they were passing and at the rain. Finally she turned back to him.

"What are you doing here," she said.

"Where."

"In Berkeley. Why are you living in Berkeley."

"Oh," Benjamin said, nodding. "Well I'm just living there temporarily."

"Are you going to school?"

"No."

"Then what's your reason."

"For living there?"

"Yes."

"Well," Benjamin said. "My reason." He looked again at the seat in front of him. "Well I'm—it's—I'm very interested to know what it's like to live there. It's an interesting place to live."

"Are you working?"

"No," Benjamin said. "I sold my car. I'm able to live on that."

"But what do you do."

"Different things," he said. "I do different things."

"What different things."

"Well," Benjamin said. "I've gone to a few classes. I've sat in on a few classes at the university."

"But you aren't enrolled*."

"No," Benjamin said. "I'm not. But I enjoy—they have some very fine professors here. There."

Elaine waited a moment, then turned back to the window. Benjamin looked down into his lap.

"It's sure a wet day for the zoo," he said.

When they got there Benjamin followed her out the back door of the bus and into the entrance of the zoo. There were very few visitors. The black asphalt walks around the cages were glistening from the rain and most of the animals were out of sight.

"Well," Benjamin said, stopping with her just inside the entrance. "What time were you supposed to meet him."

"He should be here."

They were standing next to a cage with a large bird inside it that was sleeping

to be enrolled to be on an official list as a student

on a perch* up under the roof of the cage. Benjamin turned around to look up at it a moment, then began nodding and turned back to Elaine.

"Well," he said. "He's a little late, is he."

"What?"

"I say your date's a little late. Maybe the rain held him up."

When the date arrived he walked briskly* in through the entrance of the zoo wearing a light tan raincoat and carrying a pipe in his hand by its bowl*.

"Is that him?" Benjamin said.

Elaine turned, then smiled and walked forward to meet him. He put the stem of his pipe between his teeth and held out both hands for her to take. Benjamin followed after her and stopped several feet behind them. The date remained smiling at Elaine a few moments, then glanced up over her shoulder and raised his eyebrows. Benjamin nodded to him and smiled.

Elaine stepped aside. "This is Benjamin Braddock," she said. "He rode here with me on the bus. Carl Smith."

"Ben?" Carl said, holding out his hand.

"It's good to meet you, Carl," Benjamin said, stepping forward to shake it.

Carl released his hand and turned back to Elaine. "I'm afraid it's a bit wet for animals," he said.

Benjamin nodded. Then he glanced up into the sky. When he looked down Carl had put his arm around Elaine's back and was leading her back up toward the entrance.

"Well," Benjamin said after them. "Good to see you. Have a good time."

"Real good to see you, Ben," Carl said removing the pipe from his mouth a second and gesturing with it up in the air.

"Thank you," Benjamin said.

He watched them turn out the entrance and disappear. Then he pushed his hands back down into his pockets and walked slowly around the zoo. He stopped and stood a long time in the rain staring at the hippopotamus, then bought a bag of peanuts to eat as he rode the bus back to the terminal.

Twice during the next week he passed her on the street but each time they were on the opposite side, and he only smiled and waved at her and didn't say anything. Then one morning he passed her and she stopped. She said something he couldn't hear.

"Just a minute," Benjamin said.

He stepped down off the curb and found his way across the street through a row of cars backed up for a stop light.

"Hi," he said, smiling at her.

"I want to talk to you," she said.

perch place for birds to sit on **briskly** quickly **bowl** *G* Pfeifenkopf

Benjamin nodded. "Fine," he said.

"Where do you live."

"Well," Benjamin said. "Right on this street, as a matter of fact." He pointed down the sidewalk.

"What number."

"Four hundred and eight."

"Will you be there this afternoon?"

"Yes. Yes I will."

"I'll come by," she said.

Benjamin nodded. "Well," he said, "I hope I'm there."

She frowned at him. "Will you be there or not," she said.

"Yes," Benjamin said. "I will. Definitely."

She arrived at his rooming house in the middle of the afternoon. When she knocked on his door Benjamin was at his desk reading a paperback book he had bought just after seeing her. He laid the book face-down on his desk and walked quickly across the room to the door. Then he waited a moment, cleared his throat and pulled the door open.

"Elaine," he said. "Well. Come in."

"No."

"What?"

"I want to ask you a question," she said. "Then I'm going."

"Well," he said. "I hope—I hope I can answer it."

"You can."

"What is it," he said.

"Benjamin, why are you here."

"What?"

"I want you to tell me why you're here in Berkeley," she said, stepping part way in through the doorway.

Benjamin smiled. "Well Elaine?"

"Can you tell me that?"

"Well Elaine?" he said again. "I mean—I mean I thought I did. Didn't I?"

"You didn't."

"But could you come in, please?"

"No."

"You couldn't come in the room?"

"I don't want to see you," she said. "I don't want to be in the room with you. Now why are you here."

Benjamin turned halfway around and began shaking his head. "Elaine?" he said.

"Tell me."

"But Elaine?" he said, holding his hands up beside himself. "I mean won't you come in the room?"
"I don't trust you," she said.
"You don't?"
"Why are you here."
"Because I am!" he said, throwing his hands down beside him but still not looking at her.
"Is it because I'm here?"
"What?"
"Did you move up here because I was here?"
He opened his mouth to say something but then closed it and began shaking his head again.
"Did you?"
"I don't know!" he said.
"You don't know why you moved up here."
"Would you come in, please?"
"Benjamin," she said, taking another step into the room, "I want you to answer yes or no. Did you move here because I was here or not."
Benjamin turned around to his desk.
"Did you?"
"What do you think!" he said, clenching his fists beside him and then raising them up over his head.
"I think you did."
"All right then!" he said. He slammed his fists down on the desk.
Elaine stood just inside the doorway looking at the back of his head. "Well, you can go now," she said.
"What?"
"I want you to leave now," she said.
"Leave?"
"Leave this town," she said. "Leave me alone and leave this town."
He turned around.
"Benjamin?" she said, staring into his eyes. "You are the one person I don't ever want to see again."
He put his hands up over his face.
"Promise me you'll be gone in the morning."
"But Elaine?"
"Promise me."
He removed his hands from in front of his face to stare at her a moment, then turned around and slammed them down on the top of the desk. "All right!"
"Promise me you will."

"All right! All right! All right!"

Elaine shook her head and watched him as he stood leaning over his desk.

"Elaine?"

She didn't answer.

Benjamin sat down suddenly in the chair in front of his desk and put his face down into his arms. "Elaine?" he said again.

"I don't want to talk to you."

"Elaine!" he yelled* into his arms. "I love you!"

It was perfectly quiet. Elaine stood a few moments longer watching his back and the back of his neck and then walked slowly to the center of the room and stopped. "How could you do that," she said quietly.

He didn't take his head up from his arms.

"How could you do that!" she said.

He didn't answer.

"How could you possibly rape* my ..." She put her hands up over her face.

Benjamin lifted his head slowly up from his arms and frowned at a point on the desk in front of him. "What?" he said.

"Do you just hate everything?" she said quietly into her hands.

He rose slowly from the chair and turned toward her. "Rape her?" he said.

She lowered her hands enough to look at him over the top of her fingers. She was crying.

"Did you say rape her?"

She didn't answer.

"No," Benjamin said. He took a step toward her but she stepped backward.

"No," he said again.

Elaine cleared her throat and then wiped one of her eyes.

"What did she say," Benjamin said.

She looked up at him but didn't answer.

"What did she tell you!"

Still she didn't answer.

"What!"

She looked at him a few more moments, then turned around. "I want you out of here in the morning," she said.

"No!" Benjamin said. He ran between Elaine and the door.

"Don't you touch me."

"I'm not."

"Then get away from the door."

"Elaine," he said. "I swear to God I won't touch you. But please. Please tell me what she said."

to yell to shout **to rape** *G* vergewaltigen

"Why."
"Because it isn't true!"
"Is it true you slept with her?"
"Yes."
"All right then. Get away from the door."
"Elaine?"
"She told me you dragged* her up in the hotel room and got her passed out* and then raped her."
"Oh no."
"Now I want to go."
"Dragged her up?" he said.
She stared at him but didn't answer.
"She said I dragged her up there?"
"She said you took her up there but she was drunk and didn't know what was happening."
"At the Taft?"
"That's right."
"But could you tell me a little more about what she said?"
"Why."
"Elaine, I'm leaving in the morning. I give you my word. But this is something I have got to know."
Elaine waited a few moments, then cleared her throat. "I'll tell you, then I'll go," she said.
"Yes."
Again she cleared her throat. "She said she was having a drink in the hotel with a friend. You saw her in there."
"That's not true."
"Benjamin, please get away from the door."
"What else."
" I don't want to talk about it."
"Please," he said.
"When she came out you were waiting for her in the parking lot."
"Oh my God."
"Then you ... you stopped her from getting into the car and said she was too drunk to drive home. Benjamin, I want to go now."
"Then what."
"You said ... you said you'd get her a room for the night. You took her up to it and ordered drinks until she passed out. Then in the morning you—" Elaine shook her head. "Let me out, Benjamin."

to drag to pull (against one's will) **to get s.o. passed out** to make s.o. unconscious

"In the morning," he said.

"In the morning you told her she was having an affair with you."

"Elaine."

"Now let me out."

"Elaine, that makes me sick."

"Let me go, please," Elaine said. She cleared her throat and wiped one of her eyes.

"Elaine, that's not what happened. What happened was there was this party."

"I don't want to hear this."

"My parents gave me this party when I came home from college. I drove your mother home from it."

"I don't want to hear this, I said."

"Elaine, it's the truth."

"I don't care," she said. She took a step toward the door. "Please move," she said.

Benjamin waited a moment but didn't move away from the door. "I drove her home from the party, Elaine."

"Please, may I go now."

"Then we went upstairs to see your portrait. When we got up there—when we got up in the room she started taking her clothes off."

"Benjamin, this is my mother!"

"Then I went downstairs to get her purse. I took it back up. Then I put it on the bed and was walking out and she came walking in. Without any clothes on. She came—"

Suddenly Elaine screamed.

Benjamin stared at her till she was finished screaming and then continued to stare at her for a long time afterward while she lifted her hands up from her sides and put them over her face to cover it and then finally brought them slowly back down and held them in front of her. He stood a moment longer in front of the door, then looked quickly around at different parts of the room. He hurried to one corner for a wooden chair and brought it to the center of the room, where she was standing. Then he rushed out his door and down the hall to the bathroom. A boy at the end of the hall was standing in his doorway. "It's all right," Benjamin said. He went into the bathroom and filled a glass full of water, then carried it quickly back along the hall toward his room but before he could reach the door a man, his landlord, had come up the stairs and was standing in front of him.

"Who screamed," he said.

"It's all right," Benjamin said.

"Who screamed up here."

"Mr Berry, it's all right," Benjamin said.

"Who was it."

"A visitor. But it's all right now."

"Whose visitor."

"Mine."

"What did you do to her."

"Excuse me," Benjamin said. He began moving around him but Mr Berry stepped in front of the door. "She's all right!" Benjamin said. "She was upset and she screamed! Now I'm taking her some water!"

"I've called the police," Mr Berry said.

"Oh my God."

"What did you do to her."

"Goddammit!" Benjamin said. "Now call the police and tell them not to come! Nothing's wrong!"

"What did you do to her?"

"Get out of the way," Benjamin said. He pushed past him and into the room, closing the door behind him. "Here," he said. He gave her the glass.

"What's happening."

"Nothing."

"Who's out there."

"My landlord," Benjamin said. He turned around and went back out into the hall. Mr Berry tried to look around him and in through the door as he came out but he closed it. Two students were standing together at the end of the hall and one was leaning down over the banister* from upstairs. "It's all right!" Benjamin said. "Now everybody go back to their room." No one moved. Benjamin looked back at Mr Berry. "Will you call the police back?"

"Tell me what happened."

"She was upset and she screamed. Now call the police back and tell them not to come."

"Why was she upset."

"It's not your business why she was upset."

Suddenly the front door of the rooming house was thrown open and a policeman hurried in and up the stairs. "Who called," he said.

"I did, sir," Mr Berry said.

"Look," Benjamin said. "It's all right."

"He has a girl in his room that was screaming."

The policeman looked at Benjamin. "What happened," he said.

"I have a friend visiting me," he said, "and she became upset as we were talking and screamed. But everything's fine now."

banister *G* Geländer

"Why does she want to scream if everything's fine."
"Look. We were talking about something that upset her."
"What was it."
"What?"
"What were you talking about."
"A private matter."
"What was it."
"I said it was a private matter."
Elaine suddenly opened the door and looked out. The two students at the end of the hall took several steps forward and Mr Berry craned his head up to look at her over Benjamin's shoulder.
"Was it you screamed?" the policeman said.
"Yes."
"What did he do to you."
"Nothing," she said. "I was upset about something."
"What were you upset about."
"It was a private matter!" Benjamin said. "Can you understand that?"
The policeman turned to frown at him. "What's your name," he said.
"What?"
"What's your name."
"What's the charge."
"Don't worry about the charge. What's your name."
"His name's Braddock," Mr Berry said. "His name's Benjamin Braddock."
"Are you a student?"
"No."
"What are you."
"I'm a resident*."
"What's your job. What's your occupation."
"I don't have one."
"What do you mean you don't have one."
"I mean I don't have one."
"You getting smart*?"
"No."
"Then what's your occupation."
"I don't have one."
"What do you do."
"Look," Benjamin said. "I don't think this is too relevant."
"Then what do you do."

resident person who lives in a certain place, who is not a visitor **you getting smart?** are you getting smart/cheeky?

"Are you booking* me or something?"

The policeman looked a moment at Mr Berry, then at the two students standing halfway down the hall. "Get back to your rooms," he said, waving them back. They walked back down the hall and into their rooms and closed their doors behind them.

"There won't be any more trouble," Benjamin said.

The officer looked at him a long time, then nodded. "Okay Ben," he said. "I'll take your word for it this time." He turned around and walked back down the stairs and outside.

"Mr Braddock?" the landlord said.

"What."

"I want you out of here in a week."

"What?"

Mr Berry turned around and began climbing down the stairs.

"Mr Berry?"

"You heard me," he said.

Benjamin hurried down the stairs after him. "You want me out of here?"

"That's right."

"What for."

"You know what for."

"I don't know what for, Mr Berry. Tell me what for."

"Because I don't want you here."

"Why not."

"Because I don't like you," he said.

Benjamin frowned at him as Mr Berry walked past him and along the hall and into his room. He listened to the latch* sliding into place on the other side of Mr Berry's door, then turned around and walked slowly back up toward his room. Elaine was still standing in the doorway. Benjamin walked past her and to his bed. He seated himself on its edge and looked down at the rug.

"Benjamin?"

"What."

"I'm sorry I screamed."

He sat awhile longer on the bed, then stood and walked across the room for his suitcase. He carried it back and opened it on the bed. Elaine closed the door. She walked to the chair in the center of the room and sat.

"Benjamin?"

"What."

"Can I ask you something?"

He nodded and walked across the room to his bureau* and opened its top

to book *here* Anzeige erstatten **latch** *here* door lock **bureau** *AE* piece of furniture with drawers used in bedrooms drawer. From inside he lifted out a shirt and carried it to the bed to put in the suitcase.

"What did you think would happen," Elaine said.

"What?"

"When you came up here," she said. "What did you think would happen between us."

"I don't know."

"Did you ever think of how I might feel about you?"

"Look," he said, turning around from his bed. "I don't want to talk right now. I'm sorry about everything but if you don't mind I'd just as soon be alone right now."

Elaine nodded.

"All right?"

"All right," she said. "May I just sit here till you finish packing?"

"Do what you want," he said.

"But can't you just tell me what you were thinking about when you decided to come up here?"

"I don't know what I was thinking about," he said. He walked to his closet and took his suit out on its hanger.

"You just came up here?" she said.

He nodded and carried the suit to the bed.

"Just because I was here."

"That's right."

"Well, were you afraid to come and see me?"

"What do you think."

"Were you?"

"I was," he said. He removed the coat from the hanger and began folding it.

"But what did you do."

"What?"

"Did you just get in your car one day and drive up here?"

"What does it matter, Elaine."

"I'm just curious."

"That's what I did."

"And what happened when you got here."

"What happened?"

"I mean can't you tell me a little bit about it?" she said.

He turned around to frown at her.

"Because I can't understand any of this," she said. "Didn't you have any intention of coming to see me? Or were you just going to wait until we happened to meet."

"I came to see you the first night."

"You did?"

"I mean I drove up here," he said. "I was in kind of a strange mood and I drove up here and got a hotel and got some reservations at a restaurant for us."

"You were going to invite me to dinner?"

"That's right."

"Then what did you do."

"I didn't invite you."

"I know."

"Elaine, I just came up here," he said. He set the coat into the suitcase on top of the shirt. "I just kind of wallowed around*. I wrote you some letters."

"Love letters?"

"I don't remember."

"And you sold your car."

He nodded. "The first day I was here," he said. "I got this room and I sold the car the first morning."

"And then what."

"Then I sat around," he said, picking up the hanger and removing the pants from it.

"Well, did you go out?"

"What?"

"Did you go out with girls or anything?"

"No."

"But how did you spend your time," she said. "Did you read all day?"

"No." He glanced at the paperback book on the desk. "That's the first book I've started since college."

"Don't you like to read?"

"I like newspapers." He folded the pair of pants to his suit and laid them in the suitcase. Then he walked to his desk and opened one of its side drawers to remove a handful of socks.

"What's the book you're reading," she said.

Benjamin picked it up from the desk and handed it to her.

"Are you interested in astronomy?" she said, looking at the cover.

"No."

"Then why are you reading this."

"I just picked it up," he said, carrying the socks to his bed. "I just wanted to be reading something when you came." He set the socks in the empty half of the suitcase.

"You wanted to be reading something when I came?" she said.

"That's right."

to wallow around *here* to hang around doing nothing

"Why."
"What?"
"Why did you want to be reading something when I came."
"Because," he said, "I didn't want to be just lying on the bed or sitting in the chair. I wanted to be doing something worth while." He shook his head. "I don't know what I'm doing," he said. "Where's my belt." He walked back to the bureau, looking in the top drawer, then the next one and then the bottom drawer. Then he walked to his desk and opened all the side drawers and finally the large drawer under the desk-top. He reached in for the bundle of money and stuffed it into his pocket.
"Is that the money from your car?"
"Yes."
"How much was it."
"It was twenty-nine hundred," he said. "It's about twenty-four hundred now. Twenty-three or -four."
"And you just keep it lying around in that drawer?"
"It's safe enough." He closed the drawer and walked across his room. He opened the closet door wider to let in more light and frowned down at the closet floor. Then he got down on his hands and knees and looked under the bureau.
"What are you looking for."
"My belt."
"Don't you have it on?"
"No," he said, reaching under the bureau. "I have two. I have one on, then I have another. What's this." He pulled out a marble* covered with dust, looked at it a moment, then returned it under the bureau and stood. "It was from my grandmother," he said, brushing some dust off one of his hands and onto his pants.
"What?"
"The belt. It was from my grandmother."
"Oh."
He walked to his bed and pulled it away from the wall. "What's this," he said. He bent down and pulled up a red plastic ruler from the floor beside the wall. He looked at it a moment, then knocked it against the metal frame of the bed to get some of the dust off and dropped it into his suitcase on top of his socks.
"Benjamin?"
"What."
"What are you going to do now."
He shook his head and moved the bed back against the wall.

marble small ball made of coloured glass

"What are you going to do now."

"Elaine, I don't know," he said. He walked back to the bureau and opened its top drawer again. Then he reached inside and moved his hand across the bottom of it.

"Are you going home?"

"No," he said. He closed the top drawer and opened the next one to feel inside it.

"Well, where are you going."

"I said I don't know!" he said. He closed the middle drawer and opened the bottom one. When he had finished feeling inside it he closed it and returned to his desk. He opened each drawer again to feel inside it.

"Well what are you going to do."

"Excuse me," Benjamin said. He walked out of the room and down the hall to the bathroom. He washed his hands off under the faucet*, then dried them on someone's towel beside the sink* and walked back and into the room. "What?" he said, shutting the door.

"What are you going to do."

"Elaine, are you deaf?" he said.

"What?"

"I do not know what I am going to do," he said.

"You have no idea."

"No."

"Not the faintest idea."

"That's right," Benjamin said. He looked at her a moment longer, then returned to his closet and pushed the door open again so the light would come in. He took a hanger down from the bar and bent over and began scraping one end of it back and forth across the floor of the closet through the dust. Then he dropped it and walked back into the room.

"Well what about tomorrow," she said.

"What?"

"Don't you even know what you're going to do tomorrow?"

"No."

"But will you get on a bus or what."

"Elaine," he said, "if I knew I'd tell you. But I don't, so don't keep asking me."

"A train."

"Good God," Benjamin said. He walked to his bed and looked under his pillow.

"Benjamin?"

faucet *AE* water tap **sink** washbasin

"What!"

"I don't want you to leave tomorrow until you know where you're going." He turned around, holding the pillow in one of his hands, and frowned at her.

"I want you to have a definite plan before you leave."

"What for," he said.

"Because I want you to."

"Well, do you want me to leave or not."

She nodded.

"Then what's this all about."

"Will you tell me a definite plan before you leave?"

"Well, are you concerned about me or something?"

"Benjamin," she said, standing up from the chair, "you came up here because of me. You sold your car because of me. You've changed your entire life because of me and now you're leaving because of me."

"So?"

"So you make me responsible for you," she said.

Benjamin turned around and put the pillow back at the head of the bed. "Elaine?"

"I don't want to be worried that you're drunk out in some gutter* because of me."

"Oh my God."

"Then what are you going to do!"

"I don't know!" he said, turning around and taking a step toward her. "I don't know! I don't know! I don't know!"

"Well, make up your mind before you go."

"Elaine," he said, "what business is it of yours what I do."

"You make it my business, Benjamin."

"I don't."

"What do you mean you don't," she said. "Do you think I can just ignore somebody who rearranges their life because of me?"

"Come on, Elaine."

"Do you think I can?"

"Why can't you."

"Because I can't."

"Then you're a phony*."

"What?"

"Elaine, you're a phony," he said. "If you tell me to leave one minute, then tell me to stay the next, then—"

gutter *G* Gosse **phony** dishonest person

Elaine turned around and walked toward the door. "Goodbye," she said.

"Well Elaine?"

She slammed the door behind her. Benjamin heard her walking quickly down the stairs and then out the front door. The front door banged shut and then he hurried out of his room and after her. When he caught up with her she was almost to the corner. "Elaine," he said.

She shook her head and kept walking.

"Elaine?"

"Just get out of here," she said. She stopped on the curb, looked down the street, then walked across to the other side.

"I'm sorry I said that, Elaine."

"Will you just leave please?" she said. She reached up to wipe one of her cheeks with the back of her hand but kept walking.

"Elaine!" Benjamin said. He took her arm but she pulled it away. "Elaine, I didn't mean that."

"Don't you see what you're doing?" she said, stopping suddenly to look up at him.

"What?"

"Can't you see what's happening? What's going to happen?"

He frowned at her. "What is," he said. When she didn't answer he looked down at the sidewalk. "Anyway I didn't mean that," he said.

A student walked past them carrying a book. Benjamin glanced at him, then back at Elaine. "Well Elaine?" he said.

"What."

"Do you want me to stay around then? Till I figure out what I'm going to do?"

"Do what you want," she said.

"But I mean if you'd worry about me then I'll try and get a definite plan before I go."

She took his hand and looked at it. "Do what you want," she said, "will you?" She looked up into his face a moment, then dropped his hand and walked on down the sidewalk.

"Well Elaine?"

She didn't stop or look back.

"Elaine, I'll try and get a definite plan," he said after her.

She kept walking.

"Elaine?" he said. "I'll call you in a day or two when I have a definite plan. All right?"

She continued on down the sidewalk.

"All right, Elaine?"

She turned around the corner and out of sight.

It was several days later that he called her. It was in the evening. He ate dinner in the university cafeteria, then walked up toward his rooming house and into the phone booth on the corner of his block.

"This is Benjamin," he said when she answered. "I'm still here."

She didn't say anything.

"I say I'm still here."

"I heard you."

Benjamin nodded.

"Do you have any plans yet?"

"No."

For a long time it was quiet. Benjamin looked down through the glass walls of the booth at a torn piece of paper in the gutter. When he was finished looking at it he raised his head and cleared his throat. "Elaine?" he said.

"What."

"I mean what do you want me to do."

She was quiet.

"You see, I don't know quite where I stand," he said. "Do you want me to go or do you want me to stay."

"Well, don't you have a mind?" she said.

"What?"

"Well, don't you have a mind?" she said.

"Of course."

"Then why don't you make it up."

"Well, Elaine. I mean you said not to go until I had some plans."

"And you don't."

"Well I don't have any good ones," he said. "I was thinking I might take a trip up through Canada but I decided against it."

"Well what am I supposed to do."

"What?"

"What am I supposed to do!"

"About what." — "About you."

"Well you told me you'd worry unless I had something definite."

"Do you think I can study?"

"What?"

"Do you think I can think?"

"Well, Elaine."

"Do you think I can do anything with you on my mind twenty-four—"

"Now Elaine," Benjamin said. "You told me you'd worry unless I had definite plans."

It was quiet again. Finally Elaine cleared her throat. "What's wrong with Canada," she said.

"I lost interest."
"How about Mexico."
"I've been there."
"Hawaii?"
"No."
"Why not."
"I have no urge to go there."
"Well what do you have an urge to do."
"Nothing," he said.
"What do you do then."
"What?"
"If you don't have the urge to do anything what do you do all the time. What did you do today."
"Went to the show."
"How was it."
"All right," he said. He frowned. "But I mean what do you want me to do."
"Can't you think?"
"I can think Elaine, but you said to stay around."
"Then stay around."
"But I'm having trouble making plans."
"Benjamin," she said. "I want you to do something, because I'm going crazy."
"You are."
"Yes I am."
"Then tell me to leave," he said. "All you have to do is tell me to leave, then I'll leave."
She didn't answer.
"Will you do that?"
"I'm trying to write a paper."
"All right. But could you just tell me you want me to go, please?"
"Are you simple*?" she said.
"What?"
"I mean what do I have to say to you, Benjamin."
"Well you have to say either that you want me to go or you want me to stay."
"Do I?"
"Well yes," he said. "If you're going to worry about me, then I'd better not go till I have a plan. Are you going to worry about me?"
"Benjamin," she said. "What do you think. Do you think I even would have come to this phone if I—"

are you simple are you unable to understand

"Shall I go or shall I stay!"

"I think you are simple."

"I'm not simple, Elaine."

"Then can't you—can't you see the way I feel?"

"Well why don't you tell me the way you feel."

"Goodbye, Benjamin."

Benjamin frowned. "Well, shall I go then?" he said.

"Why don't you."

"Why don't I go?"

"Yes."

"All right," he said. "I mean that's all you had to say."

Elaine hung up.

Two hours later Benjamin had finished packing. He snapped the locks shut on his suitcase and set it on the floor. Then he walked down the hall to brush his teeth. When he was finished he carried his toothbrush and toothpaste back into his room and reopened his suitcase and packed them into it. Then he undressed, put on his pajamas* and went to bed.

Sometime later in the night he woke up. He turned over and was just about asleep again when he heard somebody's throat being cleared in the room. "What?" he said. He sat up in his bed but there was no answer. "Hello?" he said. Again it was quiet. He sat a long time frowning into the darkness, then suddenly the light was turned on. Elaine was standing beside the door.

He blinked*. "Elaine?" he said.

She didn't answer him but remained standing just inside the doorway with her hand on the light switch.

Benjamin sat up farther in his bed. "What's happening," he said.

She lowered her hand from the light switch.

"What's happening," Benjamin said again. He waited a while longer and when she still didn't answer he slowly pushed the covers back and stepped down onto the floor. "What is it," he said, walking slowly across the room toward her in his pajamas.

She shook her head.

Benjamin stopped several feet from her and leaned slightly forward. "Have you been crying?" he said.

She cleared her throat quietly but didn't say anything.

"What's wrong," Benjamin said. He took another step toward her.

"Benjamin?"

"What."

"Will you kiss me?"

pajamas *AE* pyjamas **to blink** to open and shut the eyes very quickly

He waited a moment, then took a final step toward her and raised his arms slowly up around her. He bent his head down and kissed her. For a long time neither of them moved, then Elaine put her arms around him and again neither of them moved until Benjamin lifted his head.

"Elaine?" he said, frowning over the top of her head and out into the hallway.

"What."

"Will you marry me?"

She shook her head.

"You won't?"

"I don't know," she said quietly.

"But you might?"

She nodded.

"You might, did you say?"

"I might?"

"Is that so? You might marry me?"

"What time is it."

"Well wait a minute," Benjamin said. Keeping one arm around her he leaned sideways and closed the door with his other hand.

"What time is it."

"Well sit down here," Benjamin said. "Sit down here a minute and talk."

"I can't."

"You can't talk?"

"I can't stay."

"Here," Benjamin said. He walked to his desk for the chair and set it in the center of the room.

"What time is it."

"Sit down here, Elaine."

"I have to go."

"Go?"

"I have to be in by twelve."

"In the dormitory?"

She nodded.

"Well look," Benjamin said. He glanced at his watch. "You've got five minutes yet. Sit down, Elaine."

"I can't."

"But you might marry me, did you say?"

"I don't know."

"But you might?"

She nodded.

"You aren't joking me."

"No."

"You aren't drunk or something."
"No."
"Well then." — "What?"
"When shall we get married," he said. "Tomorrow?"
"I don't know," she said. "I don't know what's happening."
He walked back to stand in front of her again. "You don't know what's happening?"
"No."
"You mean you're confused?"
She nodded.
"Well look," he said. "Don't be confused. We're getting married."
"I don't see how we can," she said.
"We just can."
"I'm going back now."
"But Elaine?"
"What."
"I mean what's happening."
"I don't know," she said. She turned around and opened the door.
"Elaine," he said. He took her arm. "I mean are you serious about this?"
"I'll think about it."
"You really will?"
"Yes."
He turned her around again and kissed her. "Well Elaine?" he said when he was through.
"What."
"Let's get together sometime."
She nodded.
"Tomorrow?"
"Tomorrow night," she said. "Goodbye." She turned around and walked out through the door, closing it behind her.
Benjamin stared at it a few moments, then turned and hurried across his room to the window and pushed it open. "Elaine?" he said.
She stopped underneath him on the sidewalk and looked up.
"You aren't joking me now," he said.
"No."
"You'll think it over by tomorrow night."
She nodded.
Benjamin watched her walk on down the sidewalk and out of sight. Then he turned around and looked down at one of the wooden legs of the chair in the middle of the room. Finally he walked slowly over to the chair and sat down.
"Good God," he said, reaching up to pull at the lobe of one of his ears.

7

The telegram from Mrs Robinson was slid under his door sometime while Benjamin was sleeping. He got up in the middle of the morning, picked it up to look at the front of it and then the back, then tore it open and read it.

UNDERSTAND FROM YOUR PARENTS YOU ARE IN BERKELEY STOP WANT YOU TO LEAVE IMMEDIATELY AND PHONE ME TODAY THAT YOU HAVE STOP SERIOUS TROUBLE IF I DO NOT HEAR FROM YOU TODAY

G L ROBINSON

Benjamin read the telegram twice, once before he dressed and again after he dressed. Then he set it on his desk and hurried down the hall to wash his face and comb his hair. When he was finished he went outside onto the sidewalk and stopped the first person he saw.

"Excuse me," he said. "Could you tell me where there's a jewelry shop."

During the afternoon, after he had finished his lunch, he walked back and forth in his room awhile, then packed all his clothes into his pillowcase* and carried them down to the laundromat*. There were no dryers* available and a long line of people waiting to use them, so when he was finished he stuffed the damp* laundry* into the pillowcase again and carried it back to his room to dry it. He emptied it onto his bed and looked at it for a while, then he went out to dinner. When he came back he sorted it and began hanging it up to dry.

It was just as he had draped the last sheet over the closet door that Elaine knocked. He walked across the room to let her in.

"Come on in," he said. He removed a wet pair of pants from the back of the chair in the center of the room and dropped them on his bed. "Sit down," he said.

She walked past the chair to frown at a pair of shorts hanging over the shade of a lamp beside his desk.

"Did you just wash your clothes?"

"Yes," he said. "Now sit down."

"Where did you wash them."

"Elaine, I washed them at the laundromat. Now sit down in the chair, please."

Elaine seated herself. "Don't they have dryers down there?" she said.

Benjamin pulled up a chair beside her and sat down on it without bothering* to remove a shirt drying on its back. "Here's the ring," he said. He reached into his pocket and pulled out a plain gold ring. "See if it fits," he said.

pillow case *G* Kopfkissenbezug **laundromat** commercial laundry where everybody can use a washing-machine by putting some money in **dryer** machine that dries the wet clothes **damp** wet **laundry** the clothes that need washing or have just been washed **to bother** to trouble oneself

Elaine took it from him. "It's too big," she said.

"Could you try it on please?"

She put it around her finger.

"How is it."

"Too big."

"Let's see," he said. He took her hand and turned the ring several times around her finger. "It is," he said.

"Here," Elaine said. She removed it and slid it over her thumb. "Perfect," she said, holding it up.

"Give it to me."

She took it off her thumb and handed it back to him. "I'll get a smaller one," he said, returning it to his pocket. "But do you like the style."

"What?"

"Do you like the style," he said. "The color. The width* and so forth."

She nodded.

"Good," he said. "I'll get a size or two smaller."

"But Benjamin?"

"What."

"I haven't even said I'll marry you yet."

"I know that," he said. "But I think you will."

"You do."

"I mean I just feel like it's kind of an inevitable thing now," he said.

"I don't," she said.

He frowned at her.

"Benjamin?" she said. "I've been thinking about it."

"And?"

"And I don't think it would work out."

"Elaine, it would!" he said.

She shook her head.

"Why wouldn't it."

She stood from the chair and walked to the bureau to look at a sweater drying on top of it. "Did you put this sweater in the washing machine?"

"Why wouldn't it work."

She picked up one of the sleeves of the sweater and held it up close to her eyes to inspect it. "It's ruined," she said.

Benjamin stood. "Goddammit Elaine, why wouldn't it work," he said.

"It just wouldn't."

"Well Elaine?"

"What."

width *G* Breite

"I mean you just kind of came walking in here last night. I was all ready to go and then you came walking in. Why did you do that?"

"I don't know," she said. "I was just passing by."

"But Elaine?"

She put the sleeve of the sweater back down on the top of the bureau and smoothed it.

"I sort of assumed you were fond of me," Benjamin said. "After last night."

Elaine didn't answer him.

"Are you fond of me?"

"I am," she said.

"All right then," Benjamin said. "We're fond of each other. So let's get married."

"Can you imagine my parents?" she said, turning about to face him.

"Your parents?"

"Can you imagine how they might feel?"

"You mean your mother."

"No," she said. "My father."

"That man—" Benjamin said, pointing toward the wall. "Elaine, that man would be the happiest guy in the world if we got married."

She frowned at him.

"Elaine," he said, "he bends over backward to get us together. One time he told me I was like a son to him."

"And what if he finds out what happened."

"He won't."

"But what if he does."

"Well so what," Benjamin said. "I'll apologize to him. I'll say it was a stupid foolish thing to do and he'll say he's a little disappointed in me but he can understand it and that's that."

"You're naïve," Elaine said. She walked back across the room and seated herself again in the chair.

"Look," Benjamin said. "Forget about the parents." He sat down beside her. "Do you have any other objections."

"I do."

"Well what are they."

"You're not ready to be married," she said.

"Why not."

"You just aren't," she said. "You're too young."

"Come on."

"Benjamin, you should do other things first," she said. "Before you tie yourself down to being married you should do other things."

"Like what."

"I don't know," she said. "Yesterday you were talking about traveling."

"I don't want to go to Canada."

"Well not Canada," she said. "Other places."

"What other places."

"Around the world," she said. "Africa. Asia. Some of those continents."

"I have no urge to see those continents."

"But wouldn't it be exciting?" she said. "To see all the different lands and the different peoples and so forth?"

Benjamin shook his head. "This is nutty*," he said. "What brought this up."

"Don't you want to do it?"

"Hell no."

"But why not."

"Because I don't," he said. "But I'd like to know where you came up with this."

"Well I just think you're wasting your time sitting around in this room," she said. "Or sitting around in a room with me if we got married."

"All right," he said. "Now I don't know what brought this up but I have no intention of hopping around the world ogling* natives and peasants* or whatever you had in mind. So are you going to marry me or not."

"I don't know," she said.

"Well let's have some more objections."

"I don't have any more."

"Then let's get married."

She looked down at one of her knees and didn't answer.

Benjamin took her hand. "Look," he said. "I figured out how we'll do it. First we'll—could you listen to me, Elaine?"

She nodded.

"All right," he said. "Now we're going down in the morning and get the blood tests."

"Benjamin, I haven't—"

"Will you just listen a minute?"

She nodded.

"Now. We'll get the blood tests in the morning. Then we'll get the birth certificates. I happen to have mine with me. Where's yours."

"At home."

"Where at home."

"In a drawer."

"Which drawer."

nutty crazy; mad **to ogle** to look with great interest and curiosity **peasant** farmer

"What?"
"Will you just tell me in which drawer, please?"
"In the den."
"All right," Benjamin said. "Now I'm flying down there tomorrow night."
"You're what?" she said, looking up at him.
"To get it."
"You're flying down to my house?"
"Right. I'll get it during the night."
"You'll sneak* in my house?"
"Right."
Elaine frowned at him. "That's the stupidest thing I ever heard," she said.
"What's stupid about it."
"Because I'll just call my father and he'll send it up."
"Well we can't let them know about it till after we're married."
"Oh."
"So it's all set then."
"I told you I haven't decided yet."
"I know," he said. "But that's how we'll do it." He stood and walked across the room to the door of the closet to feel a sock that was drying on the doorknob. "I assume you have a key to your house and everything," he said.
"Benjamin?"
"What."
She turned in her chair to look at him. "Do you really have any idea of what you're doing?"
"Of course I do," he said.
"I mean you think about flying down to my house in the middle of the night and sneaking off with the birth certificate, but do you think about the rest of it?"
"Of course."
"Have you thought about finding a place to live and buying the groceries* every day?"
"Sure."
"You haven't."
"Well I haven't thought about the kind of cereal* we'll buy at the market."
"Why not."
"What?"
"I mean that's the kind of thing you'll have to be thinking about, Benjamin, and I think you'll get sick of it after two days."
"Well I won't get sick of you, will I?"

to sneak to go without being seen **groceries** food **cereal** cornflakes, frosties etc.

She stood up. "I think you probably will," she said.
"Come on."
"Because I'm not what you think I am, Benjamin."
"What are you talking about."
"I'm just a plain ordinary person," she said. "I'm not smart or glamorous* or anything like that."
"So?"
"So I think you might be better off with someone smart and glamorous."
"I wouldn't," he said.
"You want someone dumb and drab*."
"That's right."
"Well what about babies."
"What about babies."
"Well, do you want any?" she said. "Because that's what I want."
"I do too."
"Come on," she said.
"What?"
"How could a person like you possibly want babies."
"I do."
"You do not."
"Goddammit Elaine, I want babies. Now let's change the subject."
"Another thing," Elaine said, "is that you're an intellectual."
Benjamin yanked* the sock off the doorknob and turned around. "Elaine?" he said.
"And I'm not."
"Elaine?"
"You are an intellectual, Benjamin, and you should marry another intellectual."
"Goddammit!" Benjamin said. He threw the sock down on the floor and hurried across the room to sit down again in the chair. "Now listen," he said.
"You should marry someone who can discuss politics and history and art and—"
"Shut up!" He pointed to himself. "Now," he said. "Have you ever heard me talking about those things? Once? Have you ever once heard me talking about that crap*?"
"What crap."
"History and art. Politics."
"I thought you majored in that crap at college."

glamorous charming, beautiful, attractive **dumb and drab** stupid, dull, cheerless **to yank** to pull all of a sudden **crap** rubbish

"Will you answer my question!"

"What is it."

"Have you ever heard me talking about it."

"That crap."

"Yes."

"No, I haven't."

"All right then." He stood and shook his head. "Goddammit, I hate that," he said. He picked up the sock from the floor and returned it to the doorknob. "Well," he said. "Let's have it. Will you marry me or not."

Elaine shook her head.

Benjamin walked across the room and fell down on his back on the bed on a pair of pants and a shirt that were drying on the mattress. "Let's have some more objections," he said, staring up at the ceiling.

"What about my school."

"What about it."

"I want to finish," she said.

"So who's stopping you."

"Well my father might not want to pay for it after we got married."

"He won't pay for it," Benjamin said, getting up off the bed. "I'll pay for it."

"With what," she said. "The money from your car?"

"Look," Benjamin said, sitting down on the chair beside hers. "Now we'll get married tomorrow. Or the day after. As soon as I get the birth certificate. Then I'll get a job teaching."

"Where."

"Right here, for God's sake," he said, pointing down at the floor. "Right here at the university."

"You'll just walk in and they'll give you a job."

"Sure. As a teaching assistant. I can work for a degree and be a teaching assistant at the same time."

"How do you know you could get in here," she said.

"I could get in this place in ten minutes."

"I don't think you could."

"Well I know I could," he said.

"How."

"How do I know?" he said. "Because I've been admitted to Harvard and Yale graduate schools." He leaned forward in his chair. "Elaine, I have had teaching offers from Eastern colleges. *Eastern colleges.* And you don't think this place would grab* me up in five minutes?"

"But I thought you didn't want to be a teacher."

to grab up *here* to take; to accept

"Why shouldn't I."

"Because you don't have the right attitude," she said. "Teachers are supposed to be inspired."

Benjamin shook his head. "That's a myth," he said.

"Oh."

He nodded. "So," he said, taking her hand. "We're getting married then."

"But Benjamin?" she said.

"What."

"I can't see why I'm so attractive to you."

"You just are."

"But why."

"You just are, I said. You're reasonably intelligent. You're striking looking."

"Striking?"

"Sure."

"My ears are too prominent* to be striking looking."

Benjamin frowned at her ears. "They're all right," he said.

"But Benjamin?"

"What."

"There's some things I don't understand."

"What things."

"I mean you're really a brilliant person."

"Elaine, don't start that," he said. "I mean it."

She nodded.

"So," Benjamin said. "We're getting married. Aren't we."

"Well why don't you just drag me off if you want to marry me so much."

"Why don't I drag you off?"

She nodded.

"All right, I will," he said. "After we get the blood tests."

They sat looking at each other several more moments, then Benjamin nodded.

"Well," he said. "Blood tests in the morning. When do you want to go down."

"Down where."

"To the hospital," he said. "Do you have a class at ten?"

"No."

"Right," Benjamin said. "I'll be outside the dormitory at ten."

"I'll have to see Carl first," Elaine said.

"What?"

"That boy you met at the zoo. Carl Smith."

"Well what does he have to do with it."

prominent *G* abstehend

"I said I might marry him."

"What?" Benjamin said, standing up.

"He asked me to marry him," Elaine said. "I said I'd think about it."

"Well, Elaine."

"What."

"Why in the hell didn't you tell me this."

"Because it's not your business."

"It's not my business, did you say?"

"That's what I said."

"Well for God's sake, Elaine." He sat down again. "How many people have done this."

"Proposed to* me?"

"Yes."

"I don't know," she said.

"You mean more than him have?"

She nodded.

"How many."

"I don't know, Benjamin."

"Well could you try and remember? Six? Seven?"

She nodded again.

"Are you joking me?"

"No I'm not joking you."

"You mean you have actually had six or seven people ask you to marry them?"

"Benjamin," she said, "I think this isn't any of your business."

"When did he do it."

"What?"

"Carl. When did he ask you."

"It was last time I saw him."

"That day I met him? That day at the zoo?"

"Benjamin, why are you getting so excited."

"How did he do it."

"What?"

"Did he get down on his knees? He didn't get down on his knees, I hope."

"No, Benjamin."

"Well what did he say. Did he just come out with it? 'Will you marry me, Elaine?' did he say?"

"What is wrong with you."

"I'm curious."

to propose to s.o. to offer to marry s.o.

Frowning at him, she shook her head. "He said he thought we'd make a pretty good team."
"Oh no," Benjamin said.
"What?"
"He said that?"
"Yes he said that."
"We'd make a good team? He actually—"
"Good God, Benjamin. What is wrong with you."
"So what is he," Benjamin said. "A student?"
"A medical student."
"What year."
"His last."
Benjamin nodded. "And where did he propose to you. In his car? At dinner?"
Elaine stood up. "This is none of your business," she said.
"Where did he propose."
"In his apartment."
"You went up to his apartment with him?"
"Yes Benjamin."
"But you didn't—I mean you didn't—"
"No Benjamin. I didn't spend the night."
Suddenly Benjamin began grinning. "So," he said. "Old Carl took you up to the apartment and popped the big one*, did he."
"Goodbye, Benjamin."
"Well, did he have music on? Did he—"
Elaine shook her head and walked across the room to the door. Benjamin followed her.
"Where are you going."
"To study," she said. She opened the door and stared down the stairs.
"Are we getting married tomorrow?"
"No," she said.
"The day after?"
She opened the front door of the rooming house. "I don't know," she said, walking outside. "Maybe we are and maybe we aren't." The door slammed shut behind her.

The following noon Benjamin ate lunch at the school cafeteria. Then he walked to Elaine's dormitory and called up for her. She was not in her room. He waited awhile in the quadrangle and when she had not returned after nearly half an hour he walked slowly back to his room. Elaine was waiting for him.

he popped the big one he asked the big question, i.e. he asked you to marry him

She was sitting very straight on the edge of the bed holding a letter in her lap.

"Elaine," Benjamin said. "I was just—"

She held the letter out to him.

"Who's this from," he said.

"My father," she said quietly.

Benjamin carried the letter to his desk and lowered himself down onto the chair. Then he removed two pieces of white stationery from the envelope and read.

Dear Elaine,

Your mother has told me of her relationship with Benjamin. I understand she also has informed you in hopes of keeping him away from you, but that he is now in Berkeley. I don't know what the situation is up there. I don't know if he is actively interfering with you or merely calling you up or what. In any case, however, I want you to promise me you will never see him again. I am sure you have no desire to see him but regardless of* whatever trickery he employs I want to make certain you are having no contact with him. I don't think it is necessary for me to point out that he is a thoroughly dishonest and disreputable* individual. I think his conduct* speaks pretty well for him by itself. As soon as possible I will take a day or two off and fly up. I'll talk to him, then see you.

Your mother and I have not made any final arrangements yet but it is more than likely that we will call it quits*. I see no reason to keep up the pretenses* any longer in the light of what has happened. As I know you have noticed, we have grown apart from each other during the past years and this is perhaps the best time to make a clean break. I would never take this action, of course, if I did not know you were old and mature* enough to withstand it. Please believe me when I say that you are the one thing in my life that matters to me and that I love you very deeply.

I have not told them yet, but feel it my duty to inform Mr and Mrs Braddock of what has happened. They are good friends and wonderful people and it is a tragedy that their son is responsible for shaming and deceiving them after the devotion* and care they have given him through the years. Mr Braddock and I, of course, will have to terminate* our partnership, which causes me great pain since ours has always been a particularly close and beneficial* relationship.

I will see you soon. If Benjamin is being particularly offensive I suggest that you inform the campus authorities that he is interfering with your schoolwork and certainly they will take measures against him. If the problem is so extreme that you feel you cannot stay in school please call me immediately and I will be in Berkeley within an hour or two to deal with him. In any case, I look forward to seeing you before the end of the week.

Regards,
Your father

When he had finished reading it, Benjamin's eyes stayed a moment on the

regardless of *G* ungeachtet; egal **disreputable** not respectable **conduct** behaviour **to call it quits** *here* to agree that the marriage has come to an end **to keep up the pretenses** *AE* (pretences *BE*) to behave as if nothing had happened **mature** *G* reif **devotion** care and love for a person **to terminate** to end **beneficial** helpful, useful bottom of the second page, then he crumpled it and stuffed it into the side pocket of his coat.

"Let's go," he said. He walked to the bed and reached for Elaine's hand.

"What?"

"I said let's go."

"What?"

"We're getting married now."

She stared up at him from the edge of the bed. "Did you—did you read it?" she said.

"I read it," Benjamin said. "Now let's go."

"And you have nothing to say?"

"I don't like being called names*," Benjamin said. He reached again for her hand.

She pulled it away and rose slowly from the bed. "You don't like being called names, did you say?"

"That's right."

"And that's all you have to say, Benjamin?"

"Let's go."

"Benjamin," she said. "My parents are getting divorced! Our fathers are dissolving their partnership!"

He reached for her hand.

"Do you—do you care just a little bit about what you've done?"

"No I don't."

"What?"

"We're getting married now."

Elaine pulled her hand away again and began slowly shaking her head. "Benjamin?" she said.

"What."

"If you ever even so much as speak to me again I'm calling the police." She turned and walked toward the door. Benjamin rushed in front of her.

"Get out of my way, Benjamin."

"No."

She turned around and walked across the room to the window. She opened it. Outside was a fire escape and a metal ladder leading down to the ground.

"Will you quit* this!" Benjamin said. He ran across the room and slammed the window shut. "Now listen, Elaine," he said. "Listen to me." He took her wrist*. "Of course I care. How could I possibly not care. But Elaine, I love you. I love you, Elaine."

to call s.o. names to insult s.o. by applying rude names to them **to quit** to stop doing
wrist part between hand and arm

"But you can stand there and say you don't like to be called names?"

"Elaine, I'm sorry I said that. But I want us to get married. Nothing else matters."

"My parents are getting divorced, Benjamin." She returned slowly to seat herself on the bed. "My father," she said.

Benjamin seated himself beside her. "Look," he said. "This is a tragic thing in their lives. I realize that. I feel the responsibility for it. But what's important is you and me, Elaine."

"Not our parents?"

"Listen Elaine. He doesn't—he doesn't know what he's talking about. He calls me—" He reached quickly into his pocket for the letter and opened it. "He calls me disreputable. Dishonest."

"Well?"

"But I'm not, Elaine. Am I?"

"He's my father, Benjamin."

"That's not the point."

"It is the point."

"The point is he doesn't have a true picture of what's happening. He thinks I'm evil."

"Give me the letter."

"I mean he's your father, Elaine. But you should see—you should see that in this case he doesn't know what he's talking about."

"He doesn't want me to marry you, Benjamin."

"All right. But that's because—"

"It's because you've hurt him."

"I've hurt his pride," Benjamin said. "Look. Your parents weren't close in the first place. He says that. And I talked to your mother about it. She told me she never even loved him."

"Give me the letter."

"Wait a minute," Benjamin said. "Now your mother—"

"Benjamin I don't care what she told you. If you have so little compassion* that—"

"I do have compassion, Elaine. But I'm trying to show you that your father has a deluded* picture of me."

"He knows that."

"What?"

"He knows the things he said in the letter aren't true."

"Then why did he say them."

"Benjamin, because you've hurt him. He doesn't know what to do."

compassion pity, sympathy **deluded** *here* wrong

"All right," Benjamin said. "But you shouldn't—"

"Can I have the letter?"

He handed her the letter. "I shouldn't what," she said, folding it and smoothing it where it had been crumpled.

"You should try and figure out your own feelings in the matter. You should rely on your own feelings."

"And forget about my father's."

"That's right. I really think that's right."

Elaine stood and walked to the desk for the envelope. She picked it up and fitted the letter into it.

"Now listen," Benjamin said, standing. "We'll go down and get the blood tests done right now."

"You have no right to ask me to do that."

"But I'm begging you to do it, Elaine!"

"Well you have no right to beg me to do it."

"But I can't help it."

Elaine walked slowly across the room to the door.

"Elaine?"

"I have to go study now," she said.

"But could we please get married first?" he said, hurrying after her. "Then you could study after that."

"No."

"But Elaine?"

"What."

"You aren't—I mean what you said about calling the police—"

"I wouldn't do that, Benjamin."

"But what's going to happen."

"I don't know. I'll talk to my father when he comes."

"Will you tell him we want to get married?"

"Yes."

"Will you tell him there's nothing to do to stop us?"

"I'll tell him we love each other."

"You will?"

She nodded, opened the door and stepped out onto the landing. Benjamin waited till she had gone part way down the stairs, then rushed out the door after her.

"Elaine?"

She stopped.

"Will you please stay here with me?"

She turned around and walked back to where he was standing. She kissed him.

"I'll just be in my room studying," she said.

"But could you bring your books up here? I'll be quiet."

"I won't run away," she said.

"Promise me."

"I promise you I won't run away."

"Because I'd just go crazy, Elaine," he said, taking her hands. "I'd just go completely out of my mind."

Mr Robinson came the next morning. Benjamin was standing at his window looking down at the street when a taxi stopped in front of the rooming house and Mr Robinson stepped out. Benjamin stared down at him as he paid the driver, then looked up and listened as the front door of the rooming house was opened and as Mr Robinson climbed the stairs up to the second story. It was quiet a moment, then there was a knock on Benjamin's door. Benjamin held his breath and waited. The knock came again.

"Yes?"

The door was opened and Mr Robinson stepped inside. Benjamin turned around. When Mr Robinson saw him he stopped completely still. He looked at Benjamin a long time, then began clearing his throat. He put his hand up over his mouth and cleared his throat for several moments.

"Do you want—" he said finally, "do you want to try and tell me why you did it?"

Benjamin shook his head. "I don't—I don't—"

"Do you have a special grudge* against me you'd like to tell me about?" Mr Robinson said, again clearing his throat. "Do you feel a particularly strong resentment* for me for some reason?"

Benjamin was still shaking his head. "No," he said, "it's not—"

"Is there something I've said that's caused this contempt*? Or is it just the thing I stand for that you despise*."

"It was nothing to do with you, sir."

"Well Ben, it was quite a bit to do with me," Mr Robinson said, "and I'd like to hear your feelings about me if you have any. I'd like to know why you've done this to me."

"Not to you!"

"Well yes, Ben, to me. You've betrayed* my trust, you've betrayed my confidence. Do you have a reason—"

"There was no reason for it, Mr Robinson."

"Well," Mr Robinson said. "I can see why you'd like to say no one's responsible, I can understand how you might like to leave it at that, but Ben, you're a little old to be saying you're not responsible—"

to have a grudge against s.o. to be mad at s.o. **resentment** bitter and angry feeling **contempt** *G* Verachtung **to despise** to dislike strongly **to betray** to deceive

"I am responsible!"

"You're responsible for it but there was no reason for it? That's an interesting—"

"There was no personal—no personal—"

"No personal element involved?"

"There was not."

"Well," Mr Robinson said, "that's an interesting way of looking at it, Ben. When you sleep with another man's wife and you can say there was no—"

"Mr Robinson," Benjamin said, taking a step forward. "It was my fault. I'm trying—"

"Ben, I think we're two civilized human beings. Do you think it's necessary to threaten each other?"

"I am not threatening you."

"Do you want to unclench your fists, please? Thank you."

"I am trying to tell you I have no personal feelings about you, Mr Robinson. I am trying to tell you I do not resent* you."

"You don't respect me terribly much either, do you."

"No I don't."

Mr Robinson nodded. "Well," he said, "I don't think we have a whole lot to say to each other, Ben. I do think you should know the consequences of what you've done. I do think you should know that my wife and I are getting a divorce soon."

"But why!" Benjamin said.

"Why?"

"It shouldn't make any difference what happened!"

"That's—that's quite a statement, Ben," he said. "Is that how you feel? That what you've done is completely inconsequential?"

"Listen to me," Benjamin said, taking another step forward. "We got—we got into bed with each other. But it was nothing. It was nothing at all. We might—we might as well have been shaking hands."

"Shaking hands," Mr Robinson said. "Ben, I think you're old enough to know there's a little difference between shaking hands with a woman and—"

"There wasn't!"

"Oh?" Mr Robinson said, raising his eyebrows. "I always thought when you took off your clothes and got into bed with a woman and had intercourse with her there was a little more involved than—"

"Not in this case!"

"Not in this case," Mr Robinson said, nodding. "Well. That's not saying much for my wife, is it."

to resent to feel angry

"What?"

"I'm sure my wife considers herself a little more exciting in bed than you'd make her out."

"You miss the point."

"Not at all, Ben," he said. "The point's very well taken. I'm sure Mrs Robinson's technique could stand a little brushing up*."

"You are distorting* everything I say!"

"Don't shout at me, Ben."

"The point is," Benjamin said, shaking his head and holding his hands up beside himself. "The point is I don't love your wife. I love your daughter, sir."

Mr Robinson looked down at the floor. "Well," he said. "I'm sure you think you do, Ben, but after a few times in bed with Elaine I feel quite sure you'd get over that as quickly as you—"

"What?"

"I think we've talked about this enough," Mr Robinson said. He glanced at his watch. "I don't know how far I can go, Ben. I don't know if I can prosecute* or not, but I think maybe I can. In the light of what's happened I think maybe I can get you behind bars* if you ever look at my daughter again."

"What?"

"Ben?" he said. "I don't want to mince words with* you. I think you're totally despicable*. I think you're scum*, I think you're filth*. And as far as Elaine's concerned you're to get her out of your filthy mind right now. Is that perfectly clear to you?"

Benjamin stood staring at him.

Mr Robinson stared back. "Well Ben," he said. "I don't want to play around with you. You do what you want. But if you choose to make trouble you can be quite sure you'll get a good deal of trouble right back."

When Mr Robinson left, Benjamin remained in the center of his room and looked straight ahead at the door. He listened to the man's footsteps moving down the hall and then down the stairs. The front door of the building opened and banged shut. Benjamin hesitated a moment, then rushed out of his room, leaving the door open behind him, and ran down the stairs and out on the sidewalk. Mr Robinson was walking toward a taxi parked at the corner of the block beside a phone booth*. Benjamin waited until he had opened the back door of the cab and had begun to climb in, then rushed to the corner and

to brush up to make better, to improve **to distort** *G* verdrehen **to prosecute** to charge s.o. in a court of law **to get s.o. behind bars** to have s.o. imprisoned **I don't want to mince words with you** I want to speak openly and frankly with you **despicable** *here* worthless **scum** *G* Abschaum **filth** dirt **phone booth** call-box; *G* Telefonzelle jumped into the phone booth, yanking its door closed behind him. He grabbed a handful of change from one of his pockets. Most of it fell on the floor of the booth but he kept one dime* in his hand and dropped it into the telephone. He glanced a moment down through the glass wall of the booth at Mr Robinson sitting in the back of the taxi. Mr Robinson looked up through the window at Benjamin for an instant, then leaned forward and said something to the driver. The cab lurched* away from the curb and sped down the street.

Benjamin dialed quickly. The moment he finished dialing he looked up to see the taxi speeding on down the street, then turning around a corner and disappearing out of sight toward the dormitory. He pushed the receiver against his ear and clenched his fist. The phone rang. Then there was a silence. Then it rang again.

"Answer this phone!"

There was a click. "Wendell Hall," a girl said.

"Get me Elaine Robinson," Benjamin said. "Room two hundred."

"One moment please."

Benjamin glanced again at the corner where the cab had disappeared, then began clenching and unclenching his fist beside him.

"Sir?" the girl said. "The extension* on her floor is busy right—"

"Break in."

"Sir?"

"Break in! Cut in!"

"Sir, I'm not allowed to—"

"This is an extreme emergency," Benjamin said, pressing the receiver harder against his ear. "I am telling you to cut in and get Elaine Robinson on this phone. Now!"

There was no answer.

"Do you hear me!"

"Well," the girl said finally, "I'm not sure if I should be doing—"

"Cut in! Now!"

Benjamin heard the girl clear the throat. "Excuse me," he heard her say. "I have an emergency call on the line for Elaine Robinson. Could you possibly suspend your conversation and call her to the phone?"

Benjamin nodded.

"She'll be right on the line," the girl said.

Benjamin waited, listening carefully. Finally he heard the sound of footsteps, then a noise as the receiver of the phone was being picked up, then a girl's voice.

dime 10 cents **to lurch** to move on suddenly **extension** telephone line

"Hello?"

"Now listen to me, Elaine. Your father was just here. He's on his way over. He's not quite in his right mind and I don't know what he'll say and I don't know what he'll do. But I want you to promise me that you will not do anything or go anywhere with him without calling me first. I want you to write down this number and before you even go out of the building—"

"Excuse me."

"What?"

"This is kind of embarrassing. But I'm not Elaine."

"What?"

"I'm her roommate*. Elaine went out with her father about half a minute ago."

Benjamin spent the rest of the day walking back and forth in front of Elaine's dormitory watching girls come in and go out of the door. Elaine did not return. Several times during the late afternoon and early evening he noticed small groups of girls gathered in the windows of the dormitories looking down at him and once a girl came out of one of the buildings and walked up to him to ask if anything was wrong.

"No," Benjamin said.

He didn't bother to eat dinner but kept walking back and forth while it was getting dark and after it had gotten dark and the lights were turned on along the street and inside the quadrangle. Just after midnight he walked into the lobby and to the girl behind the desk.

"I want to know if there's any way a girl could come in here and go up to her room without being seen," he said.

"In this building?"

"Yes."

"She could come up from the basement*," the girl said.

"The basement."

"There's a cafeteria down in the basement," the girl said. "She could have taken the elevator from the cafeteria all the way up to her room."

"But how would she get in the basement."

"She might have come in on the other side of one of the dorms*."

"Call Elaine Robinson's room please," Benjamin said. "Room two hundred."

"Well it's too late," the girl said.

"I don't have to talk to her," Benjamin said. "But I have to know if she's up there."

"I'm sure she is," the girl said. "All the girls have to be in by now."

roommate person who lives in the same room **basement** part of a house which is below street level **dorms** dormitories

"You're sure."

The girl nodded.

"You are absolutely sure she's up there."

"She has to be."

"All right," Benjamin said. "Thank you."

He did not get to sleep until nearly dawn*. When he awoke it was late in the morning. He jumped out of his bed, dressed quickly and hurried across the street for a cup of coffee. Then he trotted over the several blocks to the dormitory and into the lobby.

"Call down Elaine Robinson," he said. "Room two hundred."

The girl dialed her telephone and waited, tapping on the desk with a wooden pencil.

"No one answers," she said.

"Keep trying."

She listened a few moments longer into the phone, then shook her head. "Most all the girls are in class now," she said, hanging up.

"How can I find out which class she's in."

"I don't think you can."

"I have to."

The girl frowned. "You might try the cafeteria," she said. "The girls all eat lunch down there in about ten minutes."

Under the dormitory was a long concrete tunnel with light bulbs evenly spaced along the top of it and at the end of the tunnel two glass doors. They were locked and several girls had already formed a small line behind them. Benjamin hurried through the tunnel to the doors and looked through them into a large room filled with empty tables and chairs and surrounded by shiny aluminum* counters*, where old men and women wearing white clothes were fitting large steaming pots down into spaces for them and setting out plates of salad and plates of pie and plates of cake on glass shelves above several of the aluminum counters. Far across on the other side of the room were two more glass doors where Benjamin could see other girls beginning to form a line in another tunnel. He tried the doors.

"This is just for those of us in the quad," the first girl in line said.

He turned into the cafeteria, then turned to the girls beside him. "Do any of you know Elaine Robinson", he said.

They looked at him and one near him shook her head. Benjamin turned to the glass doors again. Several moments later one of the old women in white clothes walked slowly across the room with a key in her hand and unlocked the doors. She pulled them back to the wall so they would stay open and the girls began

dawn time of day before the sunrise **aluminum** *BE* aluminium **counter** *G* Theke filing in*. They picked up trays and silverware and pushed the trays along the silver counter, lifting dishes of meat and salad and pie onto them. Benjamin hurried in and across the room toward the other tunnel. A woman in white rushed up to him.

"This is only for the girls," she said.

"Do you know a girl named Elaine Robinson?"

"No," she said. "And I don't know as you're supposed to be in here."

"This is extremely important," Benjamin said.

He found his way quickly through the rest of the tables between himself and the other tunnel. He glanced at the girls as they added themselves to the end of the line stretching farther and farther back into the tunnel. Elaine was not there. Benjamin walked into the tunnel and part way back along the line.

"Do you know a girl named Elaine Robinson," he said to one of the girls. She shook her head and moved one place forward.

"Do you know Elaine Robinson."

"I'm sorry," the next girl said. She smiled and moved one up in line.

Within the space of ten or fifteen minutes the cafeteria was nearly filled with girls sitting at tables or holding their trays at the side of the room, looking for a place to sit or moving quickly along the counters picking out plates of food. Benjamin hurried back and forth in the room, glancing around at the girls sitting down and at the new girls as they appeared at the end of the two lines in the dimly lit tunnels but Elaine did not appear. Finally he stopped at the end of one of the tables that was nearly filled. He waited until the girls had stopped lifting forkfuls of food up from their dishes and into their mouths and were looking at him.

"Do any of you know Elaine Robinson," he said.

They shook their heads. Benjamin moved to the next table.

"Elaine Robinson. Do any of you know her."

They shook their heads.

The lines in the two tunnels became shorter and shorter as the cafeteria slowly filled up. Finally there were only two or three places left in the whole room and the two lines dwindled* and disappeared. Benjamin scanned* all the tables a final time then hurried to a table at the edge of the room.

"I want to borrow your chair," he said to a girl seated close to the wall. She turned to frown at him. Benjamin put his hands on the back of her chair. She rose slowly and he pulled it next to the wall.

"I want you to tap on* your water glass," he said to the next girl at the table.

to file in to enter in a line **to dwindle** to becomer fewer **to scan** to examine **to tap on** to strike against (in order to attract attention)

"What?"

"Like this," Benjamin said. He picked up the knife from her tray and began tapping its handle against the side of her water glass. Then he handed it back to her. "Please do that for me," he said. The girl frowned at her knife a moment, then began tapping it against the glass.

Benjamin stood up on the chair. The girls seated around the tables closest to him had already stopped eating and were looking up at him. Then the tables in the middle of the room became quiet and finally it was completely quiet with all the girls and the old men and women behind the counters perfectly silent and perfectly still.

Benjamin cleared his throat. "I am looking for a girl named Elaine Robinson!" he said. His voice echoed around the room. No one moved. "Is there anyone in this room who knows Elaine Robinson!"

Still no one moved for several moments. Then a few girls in different parts of the room slowly began raising their hands. Benjamin waited until all their hands were raised high over their heads, then nodded.

"Will the girls who have raised their hands please come and see me!" he said. "Thank you!"

He stepped down from the chair and pushed it back to the girl he had borrowed it from. She seated herself and continued eating.

The girls who had raised their hands found their way slowly between the tables and chairs and across the room to where Benjamin was standing. The first one came up to him frowning.

"Do you know her," Benjamin said.

"Yes."

"Where is she."

"I don't know," the girl said. "Isn't she in here?"

Benjamin turned to the next girl who had found her way to him.

"Do you know her."

She nodded.

"Do you know where she is."

"She's not in here?"

"No."

The girl frowned a moment down at the floor. "She's probably in the library," she said.

"Are you sure."

"I think she had a test this afternoon. She's probably studying for it in the library. Is anything wrong?"

"No." He cleared his way through the rest of the girls around him. "Thank you," he said. "You can go back to your food."

She was not in the library. Benjamin spent nearly an hour walking down halls and through reading rooms and among stacks* and shelves of books looking for her. Finally he went to an information desk just inside the main entrance.

"Is there a way to find someone in this building," he said.

A woman looked up at him over a book she was reading and smiled. "No," she said.

Benjamin spent another hour searching the library, then walked back to his rooming house. He didn't see his father until he was almost in the front door.

"Hello Ben."

He stopped suddenly and looked up. "Dad?"

"I think we'd better have a talk," Mr Braddock said.

Benjamin stared at him a moment longer, then began shaking his head. "Dad," he said. "I hate—I hate to say this. But I just don't have time to talk right now."

"I think you do, Ben." — "Dad—"

Mr Braddock reached out and closed his hand around one of Benjamin's arms. "Shall we go in?" he said.

Benjamin waited a moment, then pushed open the door and led his father upstairs and into his room. Mr Braddock closed the door behind him and looked a long time at Benjamin, who stood across the room next to his desk.

"I don't know how you could have done it," he said finally.

Benjamin didn't answer or look up.

"Was it her fault, Ben?"

"No," Benjamin said quietly, looking down at his desk.

"Why did it happen, Ben."

"I don't know."

On the chair next to where Mr Braddock was standing was a white shirt. He picked it up and seated himself and held it in his lap.

"I want you to sit down and tell me why it happened, Ben."

Benjamin shook his head.

"Sit down."

Benjamin sat slowly into the chair, still not looking at his father.

"Tell me when it started," Mr Braddock said.

Benjamin took a deep breath. "I don't remember," he said.

"Tell me when it started, Ben."

"It started last summer," he said. "It started that night after the graduation party."

"Did you sleep with her that night?"

"No. She took me upstairs after dinner. She said I could spend the night with her."

stack pile, heap

"And what did you tell her."

"That I didn't think it was right."

"And she kept after you."

"No."

"What then."

"I called her up one night. I was depressed. I said I'd buy her a drink. She met me."

"Where."

"A hotel."

"Which hotel was it."

"Dad, this is not pleasant for me!"

Mr Braddock sat quietly looking down at the white shirt in his lap. For a long time it was perfectly quiet.

"Please pack up now," he said finally.

"What?"

"You're driving back with me now."

Benjamin shook his head.

"Get your things together."

"No."

"Yes, Benjamin," Mr Braddock said.

"Dad?" Benjamin stood. "I appreciate that you're concerned enough about me to come up here. But I cannot leave this place."

"Because of Elaine?"

"That's right."

Mr Braddock nodded. "Benjamin, I don't want you ever to see her again in your life."

Benjamin stared at him. "Dad, I can't help it."

"You have to help it."

"I cannot."

"Ben," Mr Braddock said. "I'm going to tell you something." He stood up. "Mr Robinson was sitting in our living room two nights ago crying like a two-year-old child because of what you did to him."

Benjamin said nothing.

"He was sobbing and crying, Ben. He was beating his hand on the cushion like a little baby. He was—"

"All right!"

Mr Braddock looked a moment longer at his son, then glanced down at the suitcase on the floor. He picked it up and opened it on the bed.

"You have an appointment in the morning with a doctor," he said, putting the white shirt in the suitcase.

"What?"

"You have an appointment with a psychiatrist."

Benjamin took a step toward him. " I don't—I don't think I heard you correctly," he said.

"I think you did."

"Listen to me," Benjamin said. "Whatever else may be the trouble, there is nothing wrong with my mind!"

"Get to it, Ben. Get your things together."

"Dad? I don't know if you brought a straitjacket* up or not. But if you didn't you're going to have one hell of a time getting me—"

Mr Braddock straightened up suddenly and slapped* Benjamin's face as hard as he could with the back of his hand. Benjamin fell backward, caught his balance, then stared up at his father. "Forgive me for that, Ben." Mr Braddock walked to the closet and removed Benjamin's suit. He carried it to the bed and began folding the coat. Benjamin sat slowly down in the chair beside his desk and stared at his father as he laid the folded coat in the suitcase, then removed the pants from the hanger. Finally Benjamin turned slowly around to his desk. He pulled the top drawer slightly open and reached inside. He found the money, glanced back at his father still folding the pants, then withdrew the large bundle of bills slowly, bringing them down into his lap, then pushing them into his pants pocket. He looked down to see that they were not showing, then stood and walked to the bureau to open the top drawer. He pulled out a pair of khaki pants and carried them across to the bed. He folded them and set them in the suitcase.

"Ben?" his father said, standing beside him.

"What."

"Ben, I'm wrought up* by this," he said, putting his hand on Benjamin's arm. "I'm very badly shaken. I want you to forgive me for that. I want you to try and understand."

"I understand," Benjamin said.

"I hope so," Mr Braddock said. He sat back down in the chair.

"Dad?"

"What, son."

"How long did the drive up here take."

"I left before dawn."

Benjamin nodded. "So I guess we won't get back till pretty late."

"No."

Benjamin finished packing the pants and walked to the door of his room.

"Where are you going," Mr Braddock said, rising from the chair.

straitjacket *G* Zwangsjacke **to slap** to hit with the open hand **to be wrought up** to be nervous, excited

Benjamin frowned at him. "What?"

"Where are you going, Ben."

"The bathroom," Benjamin said, still frowning at him. "It's out in the hall."

Mr Braddock shook his head and sat back down in the chair. "Ben, forgive me for this," he said. "I'm a wreck*. I'm a complete wreck."

"That's all right," Benjamin said. He stepped out into the hall and closed the door just far enough to block the view from inside the room. Then he walked into the bathroom and turned on the water in the sink. Then he backed* quickly out into the hall again and closed the bathroom door.

"Call down Elaine Robinson. Room two hundred." He watched the girl behind the desk as she dialed the phone and as she waited and as she finally began to speak.

"Elaine Robinson, please?" she said. She listened, then nodded. "Thank you," she said. "I'll tell him." She hung up the phone and turned to Benjamin. "You're Benjamin Braddock, aren't you."

"Yes."

"Elaine's left school," she said. "Her roommate's bringing down a message."

A minute later the doors of one of the elevators opened and a girl stepped out into the lobby carrying a sealed* white envelope with Benjamin's name written on the front of it. He took it from her and tore it open.

Dear Benjamin,

I promise you someday I will write a long letter about everything but right now I can't think and all I can say to you is please forgive me because I know what I am doing is the best thing for you. I love you but it would never work out. Go to Canada or somewhere I can never see you again.

Elaine

Benjamin looked up from the note just as the roommate was stepping back into the elevator.

"Come here!"

She stepped out into the lobby and the elevator doors snapped shut behind her.

Benjamin took her arm. "Where did she go," he said.

She pulled away from him. "What are you—"

"Where did she go!"

"I don't know!"

wreck *here* person whose nerves are in a bad condition **to back out** *here* to leave
sealed *here* closed

"Tell me the truth!"

"I am!"

Benjamin nodded. "When did you last see her."

"Last night."

"What time last night."

"Late," the girl said. "I guess it was morning. About two or three in the morning."

"What happened."

The girl shrugged. "She just came up and packed some things and wrote the note and left."

"What did she say to you before she left."

"I don't remember."

"I want you to remember."

The girl frowned at him. "Would you mind telling me what's going on?"

"Tell me what she said."

"She said she was leaving school," the girl said. "She was crying and she—"

"She was crying."

"Yes."

"What did she say."

"She just said goodbye and told me to send her things to her. The rest of her clothes and things."

"Send them where."

"To her house."

"Her home. Her parents' home."

"Yes."

Benjamin nodded. "Come with me," he said.

"What?"

"Come with me."

"Well what for."

"You're going to call her house."

"Look," the girl said. "If you don't mind I'd just as soon not get mixed up in some cruddy* love affair right now. I'd—"

Benjamin stared at her several moments, then nodded toward the door and followed her out of the building.

"Hello," the girl said. "This is Marjory, Elaine's roommate up at the university. Is Elaine there?"

Benjamin pushed his head closer to the girl's and tipped the receiver slightly away from her ear.

cruddy dirty, disgusting

"She can't talk to you right now," Mrs Robinson said.

"Oh," the girl said. "Well I have all her things. I wanted to ask her what to do with all her things."

It was silent a moment.

"You just hold on to them for now," Mrs Robinson said. "I'll have her write you a letter about it."

"But where is she," Marjory said. "Is she at home now?"

"It was awfully thoughtful of you to call, Marjory. I'll be sure she writes—"

Benjamin grabbed the receiver away from her and brought it in front of his face. "Tell me what is happening, Mrs Robinson! Tell me where she is!"

The phone went dead. Benjamin slammed it back down onto its hook and hurried out of the phone booth and into the street. He waved down a taxi as it sped toward him, then jumped out of the way as it squealed to a stop*.

"The airport!" he said, clambering in onto the back seat. "Get me to the airport!"

It was just nightfall*. It was perfectly quiet on the street and although the air had become dim the lights lining the curb were not yet turned on. Benjamin paid the driver then stood a long time next to a tree by the street looking at the house. There were no lights on upstairs. Downstairs the light was on in the living room but heavy curtains had been drawn across the windows so that only a thin line of light escaped down the center of each window. Suddenly the front door opened and a large block of light shot out into the front yard. Benjamin stepped quickly behind the trunk* of the large palm tree beside him and watched as Mr Robinson walked part way down the path of flagstones to pick up a newspaper lying on the grass. When he had gone back inside Benjamin walked quickly to the driveway and back beside the house. He stopped under the window in the rear corner of the house and looked up at it. Then he called, cupping his hands around his mouth.

"Elaine!"

There was no answer. He waited a moment then found a small stone beside the driveway and tossed it up against the glass. No one came to the window. The room behind the window remained dark. There was no sound. Finally he walked the rest of the way to the end of the driveway and quietly opened a gate leading into the back yard. He stepped through the gate and stopped next to a bush. The lights were on in the sun porch and through the glass he could see Mrs Robinson sitting in a chair. He squinted to make her out more clearly. She was sitting in the chair with a drink beside her on a table and was not

to squeal to a stop to stop with a high sound **nightfall** the close of the day, late evening **trunk** thick stem, main part of a tree reading or talking to anyone but seemed to be simply sitting and staring out into the back yard. Benjamin moved closer to the bush. He waited a moment, then returned through the gate and along the driveway to a door at the side of the house. Very slowly he turned the doorknob and opened it. He turned his head to listen in through the open door. No sound came from inside the house. He removed his shoes and rested them beside the door and walked very slowly into the house. He walked in his stocking feet through the dark kitchen, feeling first for the sink, then for the table and finally for the door leading into the dining room. He pushed it, then stopped, then pushed it again until a shaft* of dim light came through and fell across him. Then he stepped quietly through the door and into the dining room, holding his breath as he brought the door closed slowly behind him.

In the dining room it was just barely light enough to see the table and the chairs around it and the heavy curtains hanging over the windows. He heard Mr Robinson cough and stopped to crouch* where he was standing. He looked quickly back toward the door but then he heard the pages of the newspaper being turned and it was quiet again and he took several slow steps toward the entrance of the dining room.

There was a hall separating the dining room from the living room and by looking around the wall and through the hall he could see Mr Robinson sitting in a large chair in the living room holding the newspaper up in front of himself. Just as he was watching him Mr Robinson folded the newspaper suddenly in his lap and stood. Benjamin flattened himself against the wall. He heard Mr Robinson walking across the rug toward him but then the front door was opened and after a few moments he heard the sound of sprinklers* being turned on in the front yard. Mr Robinson returned into the house and the front door clicked shut.

"I want you to tell George to trim around the sprinkler heads*," Mr Robinson said.

It was silent again.

"Did you hear me?"

"Yes I did," Mrs Robinson said quietly from the porch.

Benjamin listened to Mr Robinson settle himself again in the chair and open his newspaper. Then he looked around the edge of the door frame to watch him read a page and then when he had turned to the next page and his head was to the side reading the column farthest away Benjamin stepped slowly out into the hall. He stopped, keeping his eyes fixed on Mr Robinson, then moved

shaft *here* beam **to crouch** to bend the knees and back in order to be close to the floor
sprinkler instrument for watering the garden **to trim around the sprinkler heads** *here* to cut the grass around the sprinkler

slowly to the foot of the stairs. He drew in his breath very slowly, then let it out. He hurried silently up to the dark second story. He moved along the railing until he was opposite the door of Elaine's room, then opened the door quietly. He stepped inside, closed the door behind him and turned on the light.

The room was perfectly neat. The bedspread with the pattern of a large red flower in the center of it was smooth and the white shades* were drawn evenly halfway down across each of the three windows in the room and the windows were closed and the room smelled as though no one had been in it for several weeks. There was nothing on the desk except a white blotter*. The door to the closet was closed. Benjamin stood a few moments, frowning around the room at the walls and the carpet and the bed, then he turned off the light and walked back out into the hall. He walked down the stairs. When he came to the bottom he stepped out into the wide entrance of the living room and stood staring at Mr Robinson still sitting in his chair reading the newspaper.

"Where is she," he said.

Mr Robinson pitched slightly forward in his chair, then turned his head to gape at Benjamin standing beside him. It took him several moments to recover, then he lifted himself slowly up out of the chair, letting the newspaper fall to the carpet.

"Where is she," Benjamin said again, stepping down into the room.

"Get out," Mr Robinson said quietly.

Mrs Robinson appeared from the porch. She nodded at Benjamin and smiled.

"Hello Benjamin," she said.

"Where is she!"

Without looking away from him Mrs Robinson reached down for the receiver of a telephone on a table beside where she was standing and brought it up to her ear. Still keeping her eyes on him she jiggled* the two buttons on the phone and waited.

"Hello," she said finally. "Get me the police, please."

Benjamin began walking toward her. Mr Robinson rushed quickly between them and stared up into Benjamin's face.

"I want you to send a police car to twelve hundred Glenview Road," Mrs Robinson said. "We have a burglar* here."

Benjamin started for her, then checked himself as Mr Robinson suddenly crouched and clenched his fists in front of him.

"I don't know," Mrs Robinson said. "I'll ask him. Are you armed, Benja-

shade material which can be rolled down to cover a window **blotter** *G* Schreibunterlage mit Löschpapier **to jiggle** to press down several times very quickly **burglar** man who breaks into a house min?" She shook her head. "I don't think he is," she said. She nodded. "Thank you." She hung up the phone.

The three of them stood perfectly still another few moments. Mrs Robinson with her hand on the phone, her husband still crouched slightly in front of her and Benjamin leaning forward staring over Mr Robinson's head at his wife.

"Do you want a quick drink?" Mrs Robinson said.

Mr Robinson straightened up slowly and walked past Benjamin and back to his chair. He sat down, took a very deep breath, picked up his newspaper off the carpet and held it up in front of him. Mrs Robinson walked back to the porch, seated herself next to the drink on the table and stared back out at the dark back yard. Benjamin took several steps out onto the porch after her, looking at her but then turned and crossed back through the living room without saying anything. He stood over Mr Robinson's chair. Mr Robinson turned a page and started a new column.

"What have you done to her."

Mr Robinson smiled and looked up over the top of his page.

"What Ben?"

"I have to know."

"Do you?"

"Yes."

"Ben says he has to know what we've done to Elaine," he called to his wife.

She didn't answer him.

"Tell you what, Ben," Mr Robinson said, looking back at him. "Why don't you come back in a week or so."

"What?"

"You come on back in a week or so," Mr Robinson said. "Then we'll give you the whole story."

Benjamin grabbed his paper away from him. "She's not—" He shook his head. "She's not getting—"

There were no sirens but Benjamin heard the car squeal to a stop in front of the house, then two doors being opened and banged shut. He looked up, dropped the paper, then ran quickly back through the dining room and through the dark kitchen, slamming his hip against a table, and out the back door. He picked up his shoes. Then he heard footsteps on the cement driveway. He raced for the fence on the other side of the driveway and leapt up onto it and let himself tumble* down into the yard of a neighbor. Then he got up and ran.

to tumble to fall

8

The next day was Saturday. Just before dawn Benjamin landed at the San Francisco airport and hurried off the plane and into a phone booth. There was only one Carl Smith in the directory. He called but there was no answer. Then he tore the page out of the phone book and had a taxi take him to the address. The front door of the apartment building was unlocked. Benjamin pushed it open and hurried up the three flights of stairs and down a darkened hall to the door of Carl Smith's apartment. Just as he was about to knock he noticed a white envelope thumbtacked* into the wood of the door next to the doorknob. He tore it off and ran back down the hall with it to a window. On the front of the envelope the name *Bob* was written. Benjamin ripped it open, pulled out a sheet of paper from inside and read it quickly by the gray light coming in through the dirty glass of the window.

Bob,

Prepare yourself for a real jolt*, old boy. Believe it or not I am getting hitched*. Elaine Robinson, the girl I brought up to your party last month, has accepted my proposal and in fact insists that we tie the knot* this very weekend. I cannot believe my luck and am, needless to say, in quite a daze* at the moment so I know you will forgive me for canceling out on* our plans.

It was all arranged in a midnight visit from her and her father. There are many strange and bizarre circumstances surrounding the whole thing which I don't have time to go into now. Elaine is down in Santa Barbara staying with my folks and I am on my way down. We will be married in the First Presbyterian Church on Allen Street in S.B. at eleven o'clock Saturday morning. If perchance you find this note soon enough, be sure and hop it down* there as I think I can promise you a pretty good show. Janie is frantically trying to dig up bridesmaids* and Mother is telegramming invitations to everyone in sight. Dad is too stunned* to do anything.

I will be back early in the week, bride in tow*, and will see you then if not before. Hallelulia!

Carl

His airplane touched down in a small airport in the outskirts of Santa Barbara just at eleven o'clock. Benjamin was the first out of its door and down the ramp. Several minutes later his taxi pulled to a stop in front of the First Presbyterian Church on Allen Street. He jumped out and handed the driver a bill through the window.

The church was in a residential section of large houses and neat green lawns

thumbtacked fixed with a kind of pin **jolt** *here* shock **to get hitched** *here* to get married **to tie the knot** *here* to get married **to be in a daze** to be unable to think clearly **to cancel out on** to give up **hop it down** come down quickly **bridesmaid** a woman attending the bride during a wedding **stunned** shocked **bride in tow** *G* die Braut im Schlepptau and was itself an extremely large building with a broad expanse of stained-glass* windows across the front and wide concrete stairs leading up to a series of doors, all of which were closed. Benjamin squeezed between the bumpers of two limousines parked in front of the church and hurried up the stairs. He grabbed the handles of two doors and pulled. They were locked. He rushed to the next pair of handles and pulled again. They were also locked. He began banging with his fists on one of the doors, then turned around and ran down the steps. He ran to the side of the church. A stairway led up the wall of the church to a door. Benjamin hurried back along the wall, then ran two steps at a time up to the top of the stairs. He tried the door. It opened. Thick organ music poured out from inside the building. He ran down a hall to a door and pushed it open, then hurried through it and stopped.

Beneath him were the guests. They were standing. Nearly all of them were turned part way around and looking back toward the rear of the church under the balcony where he was standing. Most of the women were wearing white gloves. One was holding her handkerchief up to her eye. A man with a red face near the front of the church was turned around and was smiling broadly toward the back. Carl Smith and another boy were standing at the front of the church. Both were wearing black tuxedos with white carnations* in their lapels*. Benjamin saw Mrs Robinson. She was standing in the first pew* in the church and wearing a small hat on her head. He stared at her a moment, then a girl wearing a bright green dress came walking slowly under him and down the aisle* of the church toward the altar. Another girl appeared, also wearing a bright green dress, then another and another. Then suddenly Elaine appeared. Benjamin rushed closer to the railing and leaned over to stare down at a piece of white lace on the top of her head. He began clenching and unclenching his hands in front of him. She was walking with her arm in her father's arm and wearing a white wedding dress whose long train followed her slowly over the thick red carpet and toward the front of the church. Benjamin began shaking his head, still staring at her and clenching and unclenching his hands. The guests turned slowly as she passed them. The girls in green dresses formed two rows at either side of the altar. Then Benjamin slammed his hands down on the railing of the balcony and yelled.

"Elaine!!!"

From the altar the minister* looked up quickly. The girls in green all looked up toward the back of the church. Mrs Robinson stepped part way into the aisle, stared up at him, then took another step toward him and began shaking

stained glass coloured glass **carnation** *G* Nelke **lapel** *G* Revers **pew** a row of seats in a church **aisle** a passageway which leads through the middle of the church **minister** clergyman her head. The man with the red face near the front of the church looked up and stopped smiling.

Benjamin slammed his hands down on the wooden railing. "Elaine!!!"

The organ music stopped.

He slammed his hands down again. "Elaine!!! Elaine!!! Elaine!!!"

Elaine had turned around and was staring up at him. Behind her Carl Smith was looking up at him with his head tilted slightly to the side. Mr Robinson made a move toward the back of the church. Then he turned around quickly and took Elaine's hand. He pulled her up toward the front of the church and to the minister. He said something to the minister, the minister bent slightly forward, he said it again, gesturing at Carl Smith, then the minister nodded. Mr Robinson took Carl Smith's arm and brought him over beside Elaine in front of the minister. The minister opened a small book he was holding.

"No!!!"

Benjamin turned in a circle. Then he lifted one of his legs up and put it over the railing. A woman screamed. Several guests immediately beneath him began pushing and shoving each other to get out of the way. Elaine turned around and took several steps down the aisle toward the back of the church and stared up at him, holding her hands up over part of her face. Then her father grabbed her arm and pulled her back up to the minister again.

Benjamin removed his leg from over the railing. He ran across the balcony to the door and through the door and down through a wooden hallway leading to the front part of the church. At the end of the hallway were two doors. He threw one of them open and a man wearing black clergyman's clothes looked up at him over a desk and began rising from his chair. Benjamin turned around and pushed open the other door. It opened onto a flight of wooden stairs. He ran down. There were two more doors. He grabbed the doorknob of one and pushed it open.

Mr Robinson was waiting for him. He was standing crouched in front of Benjamin with his arms spread out beside him. Behind Mr Robinson Elaine was standing staring at him with her hands still up beside her face. Benjamin jumped one way to get around him but Mr Robinson moved in front of him. He jumped the other. Mr Robinson dove* in toward him and grabbed him around the waist. Benjamin twisted away but before he could reach Elaine he felt Mr Robinson grabbing at his neck and then grabbing at the collar of his shirt and pulling him backward and ripping* the shirt down his back. He spun around and slammed his fist into Mr Robinson's face. Mr Robinson reeled* backward and crumpled into a corner.

dove *AE* past tense of "to dive"; *here* to move towards **to rip** to tear **to reel** *G* taumeln

Benjamin hurried forward. Elaine stepped toward him and he grabbed her hand. "Come on," he said. "Don't faint."

He pulled her part way back toward the door but then suddenly the man in black clergyman's clothes from upstairs stepped in through it and closed it behind him.

"Get out of my way," Benjamin said.

The man didn't move. Benjamin bent his knees slightly and was about to move toward the door when he felt an arm closing around his neck. He thrashed away. Carl Smith was standing behind him breathing heavily. His carnation had fallen off. Benjamin looked quickly back and forth from Carl Smith to the man still standing in front of the door then he grabbed a large bronze cross from off an altar beside him and raised it up beside his ear. He rushed at Carl Smith. Carl Smith stumbled* backward, then turned and fled back down to the other guests. Benjamin gripped Elaine's hand as tightly as he could and pulled her toward the door.

"Move!!!" he said. He drew the cross farther back behind his head. The man in clergyman's clothes hurried away from the door. Benjamin dropped the cross and pulled Elaine through the door and across the hallway and out another door onto a sidewalk in back of the church.

"Run!" he said. He pulled her after him. "Run, Elaine! Run!"

She tripped* and fell. "Benjamin, this dress!" she said.

"Come on!" he said. He pulled her up.

They ran for several blocks. Crossing one street a car had to slam on its brakes and turn up onto the curb to avoid hitting them. Finally Benjamin saw a bus stopped half a block ahead of them loading passengers.

"There!" he said, pointing at it as he ran.

The doors of the bus closed just as they reached it. Benjamin banged against them with his free hand and they were opened. He pushed Elaine up ahead of him and carried the train of her dress in after her.

"Where does this bus go," he said to the driver, trying to catch his breath.

The driver was staring at Elaine and didn't answer.

"Where does this bus go!"

"Morgan Street," he said.

"All right then," Benjamin said. He pulled a handful of change out of one of his pockets and dropped it in the coin box. Then he let go of Elaine's dress and took her hand again to lead her toward the back of the bus. The driver got up out of his seat to watch them. Most of the passengers stood part way up in their seats and stared at Benjamin's torn shirt hanging down around his knees and then turned their heads to stare down at the train of Elaine's dress as it

to stumble *G* stolpern **to trip** *G* stolpern

dragged slowly past over the ends of cigarettes and gum wrappers in the aisle*. There was a little girl sitting by herself on the seat at the rear.

"Excuse me," Benjamin said. He helped Elaine in next to the window and sat down beside her.

Most of the passengers were standing, turned around in their seats. One old man was bending his head around someone and out into the aisle to look back at them. The driver was still standing in the front next to the coin box staring at them.

"Get this bus moving!" Benjamin said.

The driver stood where he was.

"Get it moving!" Benjamin said, beginning to rise up again from the seat. "Get this bus moving!"

The driver waited a moment, then turned around and climbed back up into his seat. He pulled a handle and the doors of the bus closed. Benjamin sat back down.

Elaine was still trying to catch her breath. She turned her face to look at him. For several moments she sat looking at him, then she reached over and took his hand.

"Benjamin?" she said.

"What."

The bus began to move.

aisle *here* passage for the passengers in the bus